Paper In My Shoe

Name Papers, Petition Papers, and Prayer Papers
in the
Hoodoo Rootwork Tradition

catherine yronwode

Lucky Mojo Curio Company
Forestville, California

✦ 2015 ✦

Paper in My Shoe:
Name Papers, Petition Papers, and Prayer Papers in
Hoodoo, Rootwork, and Conjure
by catherine yronwode

© 2015 catherine yronwode
LuckyMojo.com

Text:
catherine yronwode

Cover:
Greywolf Townsend, Charles C. Dawson, nagasiva yronwode

Production:
nagasiva yronwode, Greywolf Townsend, catherine yronwode

Editorial and Proofreading
Fred Burke, Charles Porterfield, nagasiva yronwode

Illustrations:
Many Anonymous and Forgotten Artists, catherine yronwode, Henry Buchy, Giles
Evans, Greywolf Townsend, Donnice Rome, Johannes Gardback, nagasiva yronwode

First Edition 2015, Second Edition, 2016

Published by
Lucky Mojo Curio Co.
6632 Covey Road
Forestville, California 95436
LuckyMojo.com

ISBN: 978-0-9961471-0-1

Printed in Canada.

CONTENTS

Dedication 4

Acknowledgements 4

Pre-Amble 5

Conjure Clarified 6

Nomenclature 9

A Ramble Through History 10

Putting Pen to Paper 41

What to Write Upon 42

What to Write With 44

How to Fold a Paper 45

What's in a Prayer? 46

What's in a Petition? 47

What's in a Name? 48

What's in Two Names? 51

Is Repetition Necessary? 52

But I Don't Know the Name! 53

Glyphs and Flowers 55

Paper Tricks 55

Taking a Measure 56

Burning Papers to Ash 58

Dissolving Your Petitions 61

Disposing of Your Papers 61

Blessing Spells 62

Money and Luck Spells 63

Love and Sex Spells 68

Court Case Spells 79

Uncrossing Spells 81

Protection Spells 82

Crossing Spells 86

Bibliography 96

DEDICATION

To Sophie, Copper Kitty,
Little Chickee Wah Wah, Bonnie Blue, and Little Joe,
To Wilson Anthony Boozoo Chavis (October 23, 1930 - May 5, 2001),
To my grandfather, Theodor Erlanger Dr. Jur., who left me his books,
And to all the Capricornians, long may you run!

ACKNOWLEDGEMENTS

My greatest thanks go to my fondest darling, nagasiva yronwode, the best husband and finest book collaborator any woman could want. For all the late nights of typesetting, all the early mornings of coffee and rugelach, and all the sunny days on the ET&WNC RR in the front yard, i thank you.

Thanks to my fellow-traveller, Charles Porterfield, who has co-written his way into my life since the mad scramble to roll out the AIRR web site in 2009. A fine writer and editor, he has never let me down. If you are not yet a fan of his weekly podcast, "The Now You Know Show," do give it a listen.

Thanks to Greywolf Townsend, the amazing book designer who makes our projects look so swell. My late-night co-conspirator and 46th cousin once removed, by day he can be found serving up spiritual supplies at The Sacred Well in Oakland, California.

Thanks to my dear friend Deacon Millett, and to Donnice Rome, Susan Barnes, Aura Laforest, Michele Jackson, Miss Phoenix LeFæ, Henry Buchy and Miss Michæle for their contributions to this book, and for helping in many ways.

Thanks to the Lucky Mojo Curio Company team (Eileen Edler, Yosé Witmus, Heidi Simpson, Leslie Lowell, Ernie Medeiros, Nikki Wilson, Dave Skarr, Angela Horner, Bo Maldonado, and Therese Kimbell) and to the Missionary Independent Spiritual Church staff (Katrina Mead, Lupita Rocha, Shenique Manuel, Kelly Korte, Dani Phoenix Oatfield, and Aidan O'Ryan-Kelly) for covering for me while i was writing.

Thanks to Prof. Dr. Adolf ("That Nazi") Spamer for his documentation of German folklore, to my Grandfather Theo for showing me Spamer's work, and to Thomas Föhl, my friend at Geni.com, for help with fraktur.

And finally, thanks to all who post to the Lucky Mojo Forum, who listen to the Lucky Mojo Hoodoo Rootwork Hour radio show on the LMC Radio Network, who come out to the Hoodoo Heritage Festival, and whose kind thoughts and good wishes make life so pleasant.

PRE-AMBLE

Wearing a petition in your shoe is a well-known tradition in conjure. It does not date back to hoodoo's African origins — not many folks wore shoes back there in the old days — but the magical dusting of the feet, and the laying of tracks in the dirt for people to step over is a distinct feature of African and Black American folk magic.

The use of written charms has ancient Middle Eastern, Mediterranean, and European roots and can be found virtually everywhere that written language exists. The Jews, the Egyptians, the Greeks, the Indians, the Chinese, and many other groups have long made use of written spells.

In hoodoo, these two concepts exist independently and are also combined: You might wear a dime in your shoe for luck or protection. You might wear a court petition dusted with Court Case Powder in your shoe to win a lawsuit. You might wear a love-letter dusted with Love Me and Controlling Powder in your shoe to dominate a lover.

In 1954 the Louisiana zydeco musician Boozoo Chavis recorded a song that may allude to this — or it may not. In any case, it's where i got the title for this book.

PAPER IN MY SHOE

I got a paper in my shoe
I got a paper in my shoe
I got a paper in my shoe
What your Mama don't know
And what your Papa don't like
What your Mama don't know
And what your Papa don't like
I got a paper in my shoe

Oh, don't you worry 'bout your baby
Oh, don't you worry 'bout your baby
Oh, don't you worry 'bout your baby
And what your Mama don't know
About the paper in my shoe
About the paper in my shoe
About the paper in my shoe

CONJURE CLARIFIED

KNOWN BY MANY NAMES

Conjure is an old name for Black American folk magic practices that encompass fortune telling, spell-casting, and healing with roots, herbs, candles, and curios. It is also called hoodoo, tricking, rootwork, root doctoring, using that stuff, helping yourself, throwing, witchcrafting, cleaning up that mess, candle burning, and spiritual work. These terms exhibit regional variations and carry implicit connotations. Spiritual work, for instance, is inherently less aggressive than throwing for someone. Those who help themselves are practitioners; those who seek help are clients. Root doctors, conjures, and candle ministers are professional practitioners.

Hoodoo survived the era of slavery, but Emancipation came in 1865, and by the 20th century, practitioners had clearly adapted to developments in industry, rail transportation, and mail order sales. During the Great Migration of 1915-1970, many Black Americans moved northward and the vocabulary of conjure crossed the Mason Dixon line, spreading from the shores of the Great Lakes to the shipyards of the West Coast and right on up into New York's Harlem. Hoodoo had its origins in the South, but just as Jewish folklore and Jewish foods can be found everywhere that Jews are found, so can hoodoo and Black foods be found everywhere that Black people live. African-American root doctors in Omaha, Nebraska, are as familiar with conjure as their ancestors were in Kansas or Mississippi.

Growing up in Baptist, Pentecostal, New Thought, and Spiritualist churches, Black root doctors have long charted an eclectic path, freely helping themselves to Jewish Psalms, Medieval grimoires, Anglo-Germanic folk magic, Native American botanical cures, Catholic vigil candles, and Asian incenses, elaborating and adapting as they chose.

Urbanization has lessened some of the old reliance on hoodoo's rural repertoire of botanical, mineral, and spiritual practices in favour of candles and spell kits, but hoodoo is a cultural treasure that has not been forgotten, set aside, or overlooked, except in the most materialistic and secular of families. Just as jazz is African music played on European instruments, and what developed therefrom, so is hoodoo African magic played with European tools, and what evolved thereby.

Learn more by reading this page on the history of hoodoo:
LuckyMojo.com/hoodoohistory.html

A CHRISTIAN FORM OF MAGIC

Hoodoo is Black Christian religious folk magic, but it is not itself a religion. The prayers and Psalms recommended for use in hoodoo spells are those of the Bible. Many practitioners are regular church-goers. Hoodoo is most obviously not an Afro-Caribbean religion such as Santeria, Vodou, or Palo; it does not have priests or priestesses. Hoodoo is also not a Neo-Pagan religion like Wicca, Asatru, or Druidry; practitioners do not meet in covens.

Hoodoo's goals are not initiatic and it has no clerical hierarchy; rather, it is a skilled domestic art, the folk magical counterpart of baking, sewing, carpentry, or gardening.

Read this web page about hoodoo and religion:

LuckyMojo.com/hoodooandreligion.html

This book will give you lots of information about scriptural sorcery:

"Hoodoo Bible Magic" by Miss Michæle and Prof. Porterfield

THE EXCUSES

If this book had been written in the 20th century, there is no doubt that the readers — most of whom would have been Black practitioners who purchased it in a candle shop — would not need to be told these things, but the 21st century has brought us a lot of foolishness and culture-dabbling that has made it necessary for me to take a moment (or at least half a page) to explain that if you really want to know more about hoodoo, you owe it to yourself to study from the past.

For about 150 years hoodoo has been documented by both Black and White folklorists. It is also a living tradition, one that you can learn through personal contact with practitioners and professional conjure doctors.

If you are not African-American — if your background is Anglo-American, Caribbean, Latin American, Jewish, African, Asian, Native American. European, or Middle Eastern — please ask yourself if the study of hoodoo is really what you want to undertake. If it is, then your first step should be to make Black friends. Get involved in the community. As Professor Porterfield says, "You are joining hoodoo. It is not joining you."

You don't have to be Black to practice rootwork, but you do have to know Black culture and Black people.

Read more on this web page written for my White students:

LuckyMojo.com/theexcuses.html

FOLKLORISTS, ROOT DOCTORS, AND MINISTERS:
If you like old books, try these authors. You'll love 'em:

NEWBELL NILES PUCKETT
A White folklorist born in Mississippi, Puckett interviewed 400 Black practitioners for *Folk Beliefs of the Southern Negro,* published in 1926.

ZORA NEALE HURSTON
Ms. Hurston was an African-American folklorist. Her book on hoodoo practices, *Mules and Men,* was published in 1935.

EX-SLAVES
In the 1930s, the government funded *Slave Narratives: A Folk History of Slavery in the United States From Interviews with Former Slaves* through the Federal Writers' Project of the Works Progress Administration.
You can read ex-slave narratives that describe hoodoo online here: **Southern-Spirits.com**

HARRY M. HYATT
From 1935 to 1970, Rev. Hyatt interviewed 1,600 African-American practitioners and root doctors in 13 states. He collected 13,400 spells in *Hoodoo - Conjuration - Witchcraft - Rootwork* (5 volumes, 1970 - 1978).
You can read more about Harry M. Hyatt and his 1,600 informants here:
LuckyMojo.com/hyatt.html
LuckyMojo.com/hyattinformants.html

MIKHAIL STRABO
As "Mikhail Strabo," Sydney J. R. Steiner documented 1940s Spiritual Church practices in books like *The Guiding Light to Power and Success.*
You can read more about Mikhail Strabo online here:
LuckyMojo.com/strabo.html

HENRI GAMACHE
Gamache wrote *The Master Book of Candle Burning, The Magic of Herbs,* and *The Mystery of the Long Lost 8th, 9th, and 10th Books of Moses.*
You can read more about the mysterious Henri Gamache online here:
LuckyMojo.com/young.html

NOMENCLATURE

NAME PAPER

A name paper is a paper that bears the name of the one upon whom you seek to cast a spell or do a job of work. You may write one name per paper, one name repeatedly on a paper, or the names of two or more people on a paper. All of these are name papers, no matter the format.

If you see the abbreviation N.N. in a spell, write the first and last name of the person *(Polly Jones)*. If you know the person's middle name *(Polly Ann Jones)*, nickname *(Polly "Tina" Jones)*, or married name *Polly Jones Jackson)*, use it. You may also use the fullest version of the name by which you know the person *(Polly Ann "Tina" Jones Jackson)*. Before surnames came into use, people were identified by a patronymic *(Bill Son of Bob)* or matronymic *(Ruth Daughter of Clara)*. To use such old spells now, you do not need to research the person's parents; simply use the full name.

PETITION PAPER

A petition is a request to a higher authority, a spirit, or a person. It expresses a desire, wish, goal, or outcome. Petitions may be written in the form of requests *(May peace and harmony prevail)*, commands *(Shut up!)*, or affirmations *(The job of Superintendent of Public Works is mine!)*.

Wishes plus names *(May George Delmer Roberson love only me)* and commands plus names *(Joe Brody, call me!)* are both considered petitions.

PRAYER PAPER

A prayer paper may contain a portion of Biblical scripture that relates to your situation (Psalms 143:12: *"Cut off mine enemies, and destroy all them that afflict my soul"*) or a free-form prayer from the heart, in your own words *(Lord, let the doctors do their best for me, in Jesus' name, Amen)*.

It may contain a name and a prayer *(God bless Senator Edward Norris)*.

It may contain a name, a petition, and a prayer all in one *(Lord, bless my cousin Jimmie York as you blessed the Prodigal Son, that he may come home to us safely, in the name of the Father, Son, and Holy Spirit, Amen)*.

GLYPHS AND SIGILS

For the purposes of this book, glyphs are meaningful symbols (a heart for *love*) and sigils are signs derived from writing ($$$$¢¢SS for *SUCCESS*).

A RAMBLE THROUGH HISTORY

SCHOLARLY SCRIBES THE WHOLE WIDE WORLD ROUND
Magical spells that employ written name papers, petition papers, and prayer papers go back to the earliest preserved forms of writing. They seem to have originated in the Middle East and North Africa, but they soon spread to Asia and Europe. They are used for every type of spell work, including love-drawing, money-drawing, athletic competitions, court cases, health and healing, removal of evil spirits, reversing evil magic, breaking up relationships, sending away unwanted people, and destroying enemies. They exist independently of the development of religions, and can be found in both secular and religious forms wherever written language exists. The use of such papers in hoodoo is documented to date from the introduction of written English into the Black diaspora, but such charms probably existed earlier than that, for literate slaves were brought to America during the worst times of oppression, and they certainly carried the tradition of written charms with them into bondage.

Although this book is concerned primarily with spells written on paper, it is important to note that paper is only one of many writing surfaces devised during the course of human history. Other surfaces employed for permanent written records have included clay tablets, leather or parchment made from animal hides, papyrus, slate stones, wood tablets, and metals, especially soft and flexible lead sheets.

The more fragile and ephemeral a writing surface is, the greater the need to preserve it from damage. An inscribed clay demon bowl of the Babylonian type can be entombed in the foundation of a house, but if you intend to wear a written love-charm or protective talisman, it must either be inscribed on a hard, durable surface or written on something light-weight and flexible and sealed up in a carrying case of some kind.

Different cultures have solved this problem in varied ways: The ancient Egyptians engraved tiny hieroglyphic petitions on stone or faience amulets to wear as body ornaments, while the Jews wrote portions of scripture on parchment and placed them inside leather cases. The ancient Greeks wrote spells on lead sheets which they crimped up and buried in cemeteries; the Norse carved spells on runkafles or rune-sticks. Muslim Africans fold portions of the Quran into buffalo hide packets; Chinese Taoist monks produce brush-script calligraphy charms on paper.

REMNANTS OF PRIESTLY FUNCTIONS

Historically speaking, the earliest written charms tended to be religious in nature. One reason for this is that in many early cultures, writing itself was a function of priestly training, so no one but a religious cleric would have had the knowledge to use written language. The sacred quality of scriptural writing led to the development of scriptural charms such as Jewish mezzuzot, Germanic "True Length" charms, Koranic amulets from the Middle East and Africa, and protection charms written in Roman Catholic Latin. These religious charms consist solely or primarily of portions of sacred text; they correspond to what in hoodoo are called prayer papers.

GLYPHIC CHARACTERS

As literacy became more common in Europe, people seeking out charms often resorted to professionals who had obtained some knowledge of writing, but had either left the Catholic Church to become sorcerers or were novice priests who wrote love charms on the side.

Hundreds of written charms exist in the museums and libraries of Europe in which poor Latin or Greek is pieced out with glyphic figural characters. Whether the glyphs were meant to bridge the gap of illiteracy or to strengthen the charms with immediately apprehensible symbols is a matter that scholars are still debating, and i shall leave the debate to them.

Among the common old glyphic symbols found in written charms are pentagram stars, six-pointed stars, six-rayed asterisks, suns, moons, eyes, zodiacal and planetary sigils, the 16 figures of geomantic divination, and, of course, crosses. To these old-time glyphs 20th century conjure doctors have added a modern assortment of hearts, dollar signs, crowns, and skulls, as well as symbols from more distant cultures, such as the Chinese bagua trigrams and the adinkra symbols of Ghana.

The use of glyphic symbols in non-magical applications has become so common that entire fonts exist that consist of nothing but glyphs. Among these are Zapf Dingbats, Wingdings, Webdings, and Woodtype Ornaments. With these fonts installed, you type a letter of the alphabet and a glyphic symbol comes out — like magic. Here's a sample written first in Times (the typeface of this book) and then in Zapf Dingbats:

a b c d e f g h 1 2 3 4 5 6 7 8 9 0 A B C D E F G H

❁❂✳✴✵✶✷✸✹❍❥✓✔✕✖✗✙❖✿✝✚✛✜✦✧★

CLAY INCANTATION BOWLS

Perhaps the finest magical charms written on clay are the Jewish demon bowls, also called incantation bowls, produced prior to 700 CE in the area now known as Iraq. These bowls contain inscriptions written in Aramaic, Syriac, or Mandaic, and in addition to Jewish concepts, some demonstrate syncretic interest in spiritual beings associated with Babylonian, Mesopotamian, or Zoroastrian religions. Most are worded so as to enforce the separation of the magician's clients from intruding spirits and invasive demons like Lilith and Samæl. They are often found buried under house foundations and thresholds, where they were placed for protection.

Many Jewish demon bowls share a similar graphic layout: The writing is produced in an unbroken spiral of text. In some, the text leads the demon from the rim into the center of the bowl and traps it there; in this style, a trapped and bound spirit may be drawn at the center. On others, the writing runs from the center to the rim to push the demon out and expel it. Some are written in "pseudo-script," meaningless letter forms probably produced in imitation of writing by illiterate sorcerers.

INCANTATION BOWL TEXT TRANSLATED BY R. PATAI

This bowl is in The Semitic Museum of Harvard University:

"You are bound and sealed, all you demons and devils and liliths, by that hard and strong, mighty and powerful bond with which are tied Sison and Sisin. The evil Lilith, who causes the hearts of men to go astray and appears in the dream of the night and in the vision of the day, who burns and casts down with nightmare, attacks and kills children, boys, and girls, she is conquered and sealed away from the house and from the threshold of Bahram-Gushnasp son of Ishtar-Nahid by the talisman of Metatron, the great prince who is called the Great Healer of Mercy who vanquishes demons and devils, black arts, and mighty spells, and keeps them away from the house and threshold of Bahram-Gushnasp, son of Ishtar-Nahid. Amen, Amen, Selah. Vanquished are the black arts and mighty spells. Vanquished the bewitching women, they, their witchery and their spells, their curses and their invocations, and kept away from the four walls of the house of Bahram-Gushnasp, the son of Ishtar-Nahid. Vanquished and trampled down are the bewitching women, vanquished on earth and vanquished in heaven. Vanquished are their constellations and stars. Bound are the works of their hands. Amen, Amen, Selah."

Similar Arabic djinn bowls exist to this day, but the method of using them is a bit different. They are usually made of brass, and the inscriptions are in the Arabic alphabet. However, just as with the earlier Jewish bowls, they are laid out as traps that spiral inward to the center. They are not buried, however. Instead, water is swirled into the inscribed bowls, and prayers are said as they are moved in a circular motion, luring the spirits in. Once a spirit is trapped, the bowl is taken out into the desert and emptied, leaving the djinn in the wastelands.

For more on spirit traps, read ConjureMan Ali's article in this book: **"The Black Folder" edited by catherine yronwode**

A pottery incantation bowl in the collection of the British Museum. Written in Mandaic, it is inscribed from the inside out in a spiral to drive demons away from Shrula son of Duktanuba and Qaqay daughter of Kaspasta.

WRITTEN SPELLS OF THE CLASSICAL ERA

From the fifth century BCE to the fifth century CE, a body of written magical spells was produced in the Mediterranean region then under Greco-Roman rule. Lettered on papyrus or thin sheets of metal, these charms were made by magoi or professional sorcerers for their clients. Because they were written over the course of a thousand years, these spells, taken as a whole, bear combined traces of Egyptian, Hebrew, Greek, Roman, Coptic, and Gnostic religious concepts. Some call upon recognizable deities or demons to aid a supplicant or impede an enemy, but others seem to be untranslatable. In the past, scholars sometimes referred to the unintelligible written spells as "garbled," as if they were the products of semi-literate scribes, but quite a few seem to be comprised of deliberately cyphered language, and we merely lack the keys to unlock the methods by which they were encoded.

THE GREEK MAGICAL PAPYRI

The Greek magical papyri represent a near-miracle of preservation. For centuries, Christian clerics systematically destroyed all evidence of magical beliefs. However, in the 18th and 19th centuries interest in antiquities flourished, and surviving classical spell-books were eagerly sought out. Most of the Greek magical papyri now housed in the libraries and museums of Europe have come down to us through the hands of one man, an Armenian known as Jean d'Anastasi, who had acquired them from what is thought to have been the tomb of an ancient Theban magician or scholar.

The first attempt to assemble and translate all of the surviving Greek magical papyri into one collection was undertaken by the German scholar Albrecht Dieterich. After his death in 1908, his mission was carried on by his former student Karl Preisendanz, who published two volumes of annotated German translations of these spells before World War Two as the *Papyri Græcæ Magicæ,* known fondly to scholars as "the *PGM.*" Preisendanz had a third volume ready in galley form when the publishing company in Germany was bombed and the printing plates were destroyed. In more recent years, another scholar, Hans Dieter Betz, has worked to preserve and translate these valuable texts into English.

To learn more about ancient spells written on papyrus, see:

"The Greek Magical Papyri in Translation, Including the Demotic Spells" edited by Hans Dieter Betz

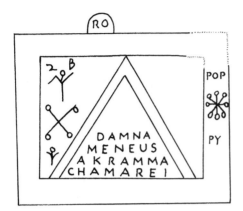

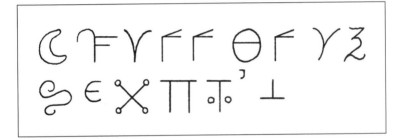

Here are three examples of the wide variety of ancient written and glyphic charms that can be found in *The Greek Magical Papyri in Translation, Including the Demotic Spells,* edited by Hans Dieter Betz:

At upper left is "PGM VII. 215-18. Stele of Aphrodite." The directions are, "To gain friendship, favour, success, and friends. Take a strip of tin and engrave on it with a bronze stylus. And be sure you are pure while carrying it."

At upper right is "PGM LXXXVIII. 1-9." It is otherwise untitled, but it comes with a petition-prayer against fever: "O excellent / ruling angels, give [him, N.N.] whom Sophie bore, rest from / the fever that restrains him; this very day, this very hour; immediately, immediately; quickly, quickly."

At bottom is "A Protective Charm Written on Silver Leaf." Silver has a long history of use in reflective and apotropaic against witchcraft, poisoning (both natural and unnatural), and paranormal intrusions by evil beings.

KATADESMOI AND DEFIXIONES

During the same Greco-Roman time period that the *PGM* and similar texts were being compiled, binding and cursing charms, called katadesmoi or defixiones, were being crafted for clients from areas as far apart as England, Spain, North Africa and Syria. Generally speaking, they were the work of professional scribes who, in most cases, used bronze tools to inscribe curses on sheets of lead. (Saturn, whose metal is lead, is the dark, gloomy planetary ruler of Saturday, a day still used for "enemy work" by many astrologically-minded magicians; the lead was considered best and most potent if it was stolen from water pipes.)

Defixiones represent a class of written spells employed exclusively to rule, control, dominate, restrain, or punish others. They address social issues of competition, anger, and vengeance. There were katadesmoi to hold back competitors in business, on stage, in court, or in athletic events; to obtain justice or get revenge on thieves; to break up couples; and to coerce lovers to have sex or tie them into fidelity.

The writing itself consists of written texts, cyphered language, deliberately unintelligible text called voces mysticæ, glyphic images called charakteres, and pictorial representations and invocations to demons and to Greek, Egyptian, and Roman transgressive or underworld deities such as Pluto, Seth, and Hekate. Some of them used very bad language in describing enemies. Some of them appear to be formulaic in composition and may derive from contemporary spell collections like the *PGM*.

After receiving its inscription, each defixio was typically folded up and pierced by an iron nail. It might be nailed to a place where a foe would have to pass, or it might buried in a graveyard, introduced into a vaulted tomb by means of a clay tube or "offering pipe," although it was not an offering to the dead in the normal sense of that term.

Because katadesmoi were written on metal and were buried in cemeteries — which archæologists routinely excavate carefully when digging for grave goods — more than 1,000 of them have come to light, and many of them have been translated. In fact, we know quite a lot about them, thanks to the conscientious work of Professor John G. Gager.

To learn about ancient imprecatory spells written on lead, see:

"Curse Tablets and Binding Spells from the Ancient World" by John G. Gager

Defixiones from *Curse Tablets and Binding Spells from the Ancient World*

Top: Lead tablet from Messina, Sicily, found in a closed grave. A: (I bind?) Valeria Arsinoê, the bitch, the dung worm, the criminal and useless Arsinoê. B: (I bind?) Valeria Arsinoê, the criminal, sickness, the bitch, putrefaction.

Bottom: Lead tablet from Athens, Greece; a curse against a thief: "... Lady Hekate of the heavens, Hekate of the underworld, Hekate of the crossroads, Hekate of the triple-face, Hekate of the single-face, cut (out) the hearts of the thieves or the thief who took the items contained in this deposition. ..."

SOLOMONIC SEALS

King Solomon was a wise judge and a great ruler of the Jews. Popular legend holds that he could control demons and converse with animals. He was posthumously credited as the author of the 14th-15th century *Key of Solomon the King* and the 17th century *Lesser Key of Solomon.*
At top right is the 7th Pentacle of Jupiter. Miss Michæle and Professor C. D. Porterfield describe it as follows: "At the top is the Shield or Star of David for strength and protection. The eight radiating lines form a magical symbol that goes back to ancient Babylon; similar emblems are also found in Norse magic. At the terminals are mystical symbols drawn from Renaissance Christian ceremonial magic that are intended to express, attract, and command the benevolent planetary forces of Jupiter. The Hebrew versicle around the circle looks more mysterious than it actually is: The text is from Psalms 113:7-8: "*He raiseth up the poor out of the dust, and lifteth the needy out of the dunghill; That he may set him with princes, even with the princes of his people.*"

MOSAIC SEALS

The Sixth and Seventh Books of Moses or Moses' Magical Spirit-Art is a magical text attributed to Moses, the author of the first five books of the Bible. In print at least since the 18th-century in Germany, it gained popularity by the mid 19th century, and the Mosaic seals it contains spread with German immigrants to the United States.
At bottom right is the First Seal of Moses, about which the book itself says, "The particularly great secret and special use of this seal is that if this seal is buried in the earth, where treasures exist, they will come to the surface of themselves, without any presence during a Full Moon."

JEWISH GRIMOIRE MAGIC IN OBEAH AND HOODOO

Solomonic and Mosaic seals have been used by African-American root doctors and Afro-West-Indian obeah practitioners since the 19th century. *The Sixth and Seventh Books of Moses* was banned in Jamaica, adding to its popularity. Harry M. Hyatt interviewed root doctors who worked with these seals in the 1930s. They are still used in mojo bags and set under candles. Most candle shops stock both King Solomon Wisdom Oil and Moses Oil.
Read more about Solomonic and Mosaic magic in conjure in this book:
"Hoodoo Bible Magic" by Miss Michæle and Prof. C. D. Porterfield

CALLIGRAMS AND MICROCALLIGRAPHY

A calligram is a picture made of alphabetic characters or cyphered text. Crafting these images is a popular art form in Jewish and Islamic cultures.

Microcalligraphy, also known as micrography or miniature writing, is a form of calligram that employs very small writing to produce larger images. Viewed from a distance, each line simply looks like a pen-stroke. However, upon close examination, it proves to be meaningful text, generally a well-known prayer or a commentary upon the picture. Microcalligraphy as a magical art form is attributed to Jewish sources.

Jewish custom holds that, even after the invention of moveable type, the sacred books of the Tanakh should continue to be hand-written as scrolls, and that these scrolls should be perfect, with no blot of mistake on them. A person who trains to write out Hebrew Biblical scrolls, prayer-papers that go inside of protective mezuzah cases, and tefillin that are worn on the body while at prayer, is called a sofer or scribe.

Sofers may also design and write out ornamental ketubah marriage contracts and gittin divorce documents. These are inscribed in Aramaic, the common language of the Jews for about 3,000 years, and the language that Jesus spoke. Aramaic continues to be used on non-sacred texts that have significance as Jewish cultural objects.

Jewish calligram: Psalms 91 as a Menorah; Arabic calligram: Pea-Hen.

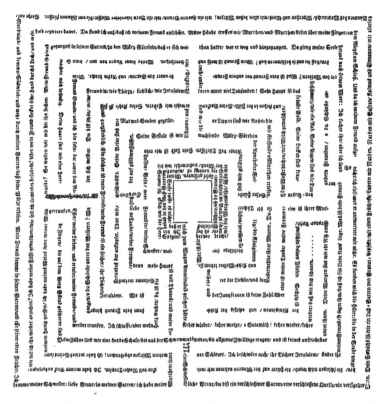

From *Die Deutsche Volkskunde* by Adolf Spamer: An 18th century Jewish "Schriftlabyrinth als Hochzeitsgabe" (literary labyrinth as wedding task). Finding a path through the maze symbolizes sexual union. The typeset walls are comprised of the text of the Song of Solomon 4:12 - 6:12:

"*A garden inclosed is my sister, my spouse; a spring shut up, a fountain sealed. Thy plants are an orchard of pomegranates, with pleasant fruits; camphire, with spikenard; spikenard and saffron; calamus and cinnamon, with all trees of frankincense; myrrh and aloes, with all the chief spices: A fountain of gardens, a well of living waters, and streams from Lebanon.*"

"*Awake, O north wind; and come, thou south; blow upon my garden, that the spices thereof may flow out. Let my beloved come into his garden, and eat his pleasant fruits.*"

"*I am come into my garden, my sister, my spouse: I have gathered my myrrh with my spice; I have eaten my honeycomb with my honey ...*"

During the era of Enlightenment, Ashkenazi Jewish sofers not only perfected their Hebrew and Aramaic magical calligraphy, they also used the Latin alphabet, and eventually, as printers, they created novel forms of ornamental and magical typesetting, which retained a sacred, mystical, kabbalistic, and Biblical character. Meanwhile, secular calligraphic pieces were produced as memorials, commemorations, or gifts of honour to important personages, and the practice of lettering these passed into German Christian hands as well.

The typewriter was invented in the 19th century and its use of fixed-width fonts, in which every letter from an I to an M has exactly the same width, led to the development of typewriter art. After the invention of the computer, this became known as ASCII art, due to the use of the American Standard Code for Information Interchange in early internet applications. Many people think that ASCII art originated with the computer, but such is not the case. Examples of typewriter art from Germany in the 1930s show the same kind of inventiveness seen in usenet posts from the 1990s to the present. In the current era of copy-paste digital type, the amount of time and effort that goes into the production of a personally illustrated typewriter art signature-block is no longer well appreciated or even understood, but such a piece of work, typed onto paper, is as personal as the sender's handwriting, and as useful in magic.

A detail of the portrait at right, showing that portions of the picture are made up of words.

```
     ..ed$$$$be..
    .d$$$$$$$$$$$$$$c
  .$$$$P""  $$$  ""*$$$$c
  z$$$*"    $$$    *$$$e
  z$$$"     $$$    ^$$$L
 .$$$F      $$$     '$$$.
 4$$$      d$$$$.    $$$F
 4$$$    .$$$$$$$e   $$$F
 '$$$r  d$$P$$$$$$$.  .$$$"
 *$$$..$$$"  $$$  "$$$e $$$P
  *$$$$$P"   $$$  ^*$$$$$$
  *$$$c.     $$$  .z$$$$P
   ^*$$$$$$$$$$$$$$$$$P"
    "*$$$$$$$$$*""
      """"     Gilo94'
```

ASCII peace symbol signature devised by the British usenet poster Giles Evans in 1994.

From *Die Deutsche Volkskunde* by Adolf Spamer: The young Holy Roman Emperor Joseph I (1678-1711), King of Germany, Hungary, Bohemia, Dalmatia, Croatia, Slavonia, Rama, Serbia, Galicia, Lodomeria, Cumania and Bulgaria. This ink-on-parchment portrait was made between 1687, when he was crowned King of Hungary at age nine, and 1690, when he became King in Germany at age eleven. The hair, crown, and scepter are words, the rest is conventional line-art. See the page at left for a detail.

THE TRUE LENGTH

"True length" or "holy length" charms are a feature of Austrian and Bavarian religious Catholic folk magic. The interest in these lengths is founded upon Ephesians 3:17-19, in which Paul prays, *"that Christ may dwell in your hearts by faith; that ye, being rooted and grounded in love, may be able to comprehend with all saints what is the breadth, and length, and depth, and height; and to know the love of Christ, which passeth knowledge, that ye might be filled with all the fulness of God."* Some scholars date these true lengths to the Middle Ages. The earliest were fixed spaces — the width of a doorway, for instance. They bear signs warranting that they represent the "true length" of a Biblical or canonized person, or a fraction thereof, such as "one-sixth the length of Christ." The form shown here, wood-blocks printed on paper, dates to the 1750s.

The true length of Holy Mother Mary was far more popular in Bavaria and Austria than the true length of Jesus. The home in Loreto, Italy, where Mary was said to have lived out her days after fleeing the destruction of Jerusalem, was a place of pilgrimage that had her true length, as well as the length of her foot. Pilgrims returning to Bavaria and Austria from Loreto brought silk ribbons bearing these exact measures and testified that they wrought miraculous cures and assistance of all kinds. The similarity between these ribbons and the cords distributed to pilgrims at the grave of Mary's namesake Miriam the Prophetess ought not to go unnoticed.

Ribbon-lengths were copied to parchment and the accounts of miracles were written on the parchment: In brief, you are to recite the Ave Maria 63 times (the number of years Mary lived, that is, the true length of her life) on Mary's feast-days. You may carry the charm or keep it in your home to receive grace and other benefits now and forever. If a woman in labour lays down with the length of Our Lady Mary, Queen of Heaven, running from head to foot and between her breasts, she will have a safe delivery.

By the 18th century, true lengths printed on paper were available in several variations A Mary-Length chapel in Regensburg housed a true-length statue of Mary, and the papers were sold there to pilgrims. In 1908, a Munich printer published folded true lengths on blue paper, from which the version here derives, via *Die Deutsche Volkskunde* by Adolf Spamer.

To make your own true length, photocopy the 12 panels at 100% size and paste or glue them together into a long strip, about 5 feet long. Panels 1 through 11 are Mary's length; panel 12 is the length of her foot-track.

Panel 1

Gewisse wahrhafte rechte Läng und Dicke unser lieben Frauen, und der übergebenedeyten Himmels-Königinn

M A R I A,

welche heilige Läng zwar aus seidenen Banden den Pilgramen, welche das heilige Haus zu Loretto besuchen, mitgetheilt worden.

Panel 2

Wann ein Manns- oder Weibsperson eine solch heilige Läng bey sich tragt oder in seiner Behausung hat, der wird absonderliche Gnaden von unser lieben Frauen zu gewarten haben, nicht allein hier zeitlich, sondern dort ewig. Man muß aber auf das wenigste dieselbe alle heilige Frauenfest mit Andacht beten, welche aber nicht lesen können, sollen alle Frauenfest 63 Ave Maria beten, zu Ehren unser Frauen-Alter und ihrer heiligen Läng, absonderlich aber sollen ihnen die schwangere Frauen lassen anempfohlen seyn, wanns eine Frau, so in den Kindsnöthen ist, mit Andacht bethet, die wird absonderliche Hülf und Beystand von unser lieben Frauen zu gewarten haben. Jetzt

✝ SHI Jetzt heben sich an die schönen Grüß und Gebether, so von einem frommen unser lieben Frauen andächtigen Liebhaber hiebeygelegt, wer nun diese Andacht mit Eifer bethet, der wird gewißlich von der seligsten Mutter Gottes eine große Gnad und Beystand verspüren, absonderlich in der Stund seines letzten Endes.

Hundert tausendmal sey gegrüßt durch die Allmacht Gott des Vaters, du jungfräuliches Herz Mariä vor der Geburt. Hundert tausendmal sey gegrüßt durch die Geburt, Leben, Leiden, Sterben, Auferstehung, und Himmelfahrt deines lieben Sohns, du jungfräuliches Herz Mariä in der Geburt. Hun-

Panel 3

dert tausendmal sey gegrüßt durch die Lieb des heiligen Geistes, jungfräuliches Herz Mariä nach der Geburt. Hundert tausendmal sey gegrüßt durch deine heilige Lang du Lustgarten der allerheiligsten Dreyfaltigkeit. Gebenedeyet sey deine heilige Geburt. Hochgepriesen sey deine heilige Aufopferung in dem Tempel. Hochlobwürdig sey deine Verkündigung. Zu loben und zu preisen deine Heimsuchung. Glorificirt, triumphirt deine glorwürdigste Himmelfahrt. Lob-und Preiswürdig deine heil. Läng heil. Maria! gebenedeyt sey dein heiliges Haupt,- das von der heiligsten Dreyfaltigkeit gekrönet worden. Gebenedeyet seyen deine heil. Augen, welche das Kind-

Panel 4

Kindlein Jesum in der Menschheit zum ersten angeschauet. Gebenedeyet seyen deine heil. Ohren, die so oft mit dem englischen Lobgesang erfüllet gewesen. Gebenedeyet seyen deine heilige Lefzen, die das Kindlein Jesum so oft geküßt. Gebenedeyt sey dein heiliger Mund, der das Kindlein so oft geliebt. Gebenedeyt seyen deine heilige Händ, die so würdig gewesen das Kindlein Jesu zum ersten zu dienen. Gebenedeyt seyen deine heilige Arm, so das Kindlein Jesu so oft herzinniglich umfangen. Gebenedeyt seyen deine heilige Brüst, die das Kindlein Jesum so oft berührt. Gebenedeyt sey dein gebenedeytes Herz, das ohne Unterlaß gegen deinen liebsten Sohn gebrunnen. Gebenedeyt sey deine heilige Schooß,

darin das Kindlein Jesu so oft süßiglich geschlafen. Gebenedeyet seyen deine heilige Knie, die sich so oft im Gebeth gebogen. Gebenedeyet seyen deine heilige Füß, so 63 Jahr so viele harte Tritt gegangen. Gebenedeyt sey dein heiliger Leib, darinnen das ewige Wort 8 Monat so süßiglich geruhet. Gebenedeyt sey deine heilige Läng, so Gott vom Anfang wohl gefallen. Gebenedeyt sey deine heilige Läng, daran sich die Engel belustigen. Glorificirt sey deine heilige Läng in alle Ewigkeit, Amen.

Eine

Eine schöne Befehung in die Läng Mariä.

Heilige Maria! ich befehle mich u die meinige sammt meiner Freundschaft in deine heilige Läng, daß du uns beschützt vor des Teufels Anlauf, vor Feuer=und Wassernoth, vor Armuth, Sünd und Schanden, vor Diebstahl, Kett und Banden. Heil. Maria! ich befehle mich heut u allezeit in deine heil. Läng, auf daß deine heil. Läng mein Schutz und Zuflucht sey. Deine heil. Läng sey mein Deckmantel und Schild wider alle meine Feind, ich fehle mich heut und allezeit, Kraft deiner heil. Läng in alle heil. Meßopfer, damit, in Kraft selbiger Wort beschützet werde. Ich befehle mich heut und allezeit mit L und Seel, mein Herz und Mund, sammt al-

Panel 7

len was mir zuständig, Sinn und Leben, Ehr und Gut, Verstand und Willen, Gedächtniß und Anmuthung, inner und äußerliches in deine heil. Läng, Schutz und Schirm, auf daß du mich in deine mütterliche Barmherzigkeit beschützest und beschirmest vor allen Unglück, Eisen und Waßen, vor geistlichen und leiblichen Fall, vor Band und Gefängniß, vor Gift und allen bösen Nachstellungen, vor Kugel und Pfeil, vor Zauberey und allen Schrecken, vor ungerechten Urtheil, und Nachstellungen der Feinden, vor falschen Zungen, Ohrabschneidung, und Afterreden, und all andern Uebel, so mit an Leib und Seel schaden mögen, dich erinnere

Panel 8

dich durch deine heil. Läng, o Maria! daß heut und allezeit wollest zu Ruhe stellen, befriedigen und hemmen alle böse übel nachredende Zungen, alle falsche Herzen, so mir schaden können, oder zu schaden begehren, auf daß sie mir weder an Seel und Leib, noch Gütern und Leben, auch in meinen Lob nicht schaden können. O heilige Maria! durch deine Demuth, und heilige Läng, stille und befriedige alle unruhige Zungen und Herzen, so mir zu schaden begehren, und bitte, o Maria! durch deine heilige Läng, mache kraftlos aller meiner Feinden und Widersacher Zungen, Herzen, Hände und Bemühungen, auf daß sie weder geistlich noch leiblich etwas wider mich vermögen, viel

Panel 9

weniger Rath geben, oder schaden können, die du nun lebest glorwürdig und sicher im Himmel, in Ewigkeit, Amen.

Heilige Maria, deine heil. Läng erfreue mich, deine heil. Läng erquicke mich, deine heil. Läng stärke mich, deine heil. Läng ehre ich, deine heil. Läng bene-deye ich, bis ich dich mit Freuden sehe in deiner Glorie ewiglich, Amen.

Zu dem Beschluß.

O Maria mein, die Läng dein, ist ja mein Freud auf Erden, mein Trost und mein Begierd, mein Hoffnung selig zu werden.

Auf-

Panel 10

Panel 11

Aufopferung in die heilige Läng.

O Mutter Gottes der Engel Zier, dieses Gebeth nimm an von mir, so ich in deiner Läng gebethen, hilf mir doch aus allen Nöthen, die nimm zu deiner Gab von mir, nichts anders kann ich geben dir, befehl mich deinem Kind allzeit, an mein End sey von mir nicht weit, hilf mir die bösen Geister hemmen, meine arme Seel du wollest nehmen, und solche stellen vor dein Sohn, der für uns alle hat genug gethan, damit ich nach dem Jammerthal, dort wohnen mög in Himmels-Saal, Amen. † † †

Panel 12

Das ist das rechte wahrhaftige Maaß des Fuß unser lieben Frauen, welche aufbehalten wird in Hispanien in einem Kloster. Durch deine heilige Jungfrauschaft und unbefleckte Empfängniß, o reinste Jungfrau Maria! reinige mein Herz Leib und Seel, Amen.

INDIAN AND HIMALAYAN WRITTEN AMULETS

Block-printed prayers stamped on paper or cloth, are a feature of Vajrayana Buddhism in Tibet, Bhutan, and Nepal. Cloth blocks are sewn to cords and flutter in the wind in the form of prayer flags. Paper sheets like the one shown here are thrown into the wind to spread blessings. Papers may also be folded into flat packets and covered with woven patterns of embroidery floss.

Text prayers are placed into prayer wheels where they are wrapped around spindles inside wooden or metal cases, and spun by means of a crank to activate the prayer.

Metal cases, called kavachas in India and gaus in Tibet, hold written and glyphic prayers and wishes; they are worn as jewelry. In Mongolia, similar Vajrayana prayers are printed on small pieces of cloth and folded into flat brocade packets to be worn in one's clothing for protection.

THE GERMAN POW WOW TRADITION IN AMERICA

The Long Lost Friend or *Der Lange Verborgene Freund* is a magical German receipt-book by Johann Georg Hohman, published in Pennsylvania in 1820. Since the 1880s, it has been known in English as *Pow Wows* and the author as "John George" Hohman. Highly popular among Black hoodoo practitioners, it abounds with paper spells, such as the following:

TO CURE A FEVER

Write these words on paper, wrap the paper in a large Plantain leaf, lay it on the navel of a person afflicted with fever, and the illness will soon depart.

Potmat Sineat
Potmat Sineat
Potmat Sineat

Read more about German folk magic in America here:
"Pow Wows or The Long Lost Friend" by John George Hohman
LuckyMojo.com/powwows.html

WITTENBERG LETTERS

Similar to the German spells found in *Pow Wows or The Long Lost Friend* are the Scandinavian spells of trolldom folk magic. Some of these use papers written in garbled Latin, which Swedish folk magicians call "Wittenberg letters." As Johannes Gardback wrote in his book on trolldom, Wittenberg is "a German town in which Scandinavian priests studied theology. It is associated with magic, the Jewish kabbalah, and folkloric legends connected to trolldom, magical words, and black arts books.

"The Wittenberg legend is supported by the fact that astrology, magic, kabbalah, demonology, and similar arts were taught within the grand subject of theology at the university. The town of Wittenberg is also associated with the legendary German magician Doctor Faust and the Höllenzwang grimoire attributed to him, so the legends of black books from Wittenberg have some grounding in the popular imagination.

"In old Scandinavia, priests who practiced trolldom (a not-uncommon custom at the time) were called Wittenbergspräster (priests of Wittenberg) and magical symbols, letters, and spoken formulas were known as Wittenbergska tecken (Wittenberg symbols), Wittenbergska bokstäver (Wittenberg letters), or Wittenbergska character (Wittenberg characters). These usually refer to Hebrew letters or words, taken from the kabbalah, or to Jewish symbols like those seen in Mosaic and Solomonic grimoires.

"A written talisman or troll letter for protection is called a svärdsbrev (sword letter) or värnebrev (guardian letter). These are usually written by a professional and bought by the person who wishes to be protected."

Here are some spells that utilize Wittenberg letters:

TO GET A MAIDEN TO LIFT HER SHIRT FOR YOU

Write the following Wittenberg words on a piece of parchment and place it under the threshold, then she will take up her clothes.

Amista Asterit

(Norway, 18th century)

TO MAKE A PERSON DANCE AGAINST THEIR WILL

Take some blood from a bat, write these Wittenberg words on a piece of paper, and place it under the threshold.

Pela Amon Ole Satorum Lentum Ovins

(Norway, 18th century)

A SVÄRDSBREV

Sofa manða be sefu os sbra svises sen gabet febent
ðastet sofufux guaviex simuk ufmerum somnit sef fifesupas
fevencof suef Ð bemuft seara sirosta nafo aabi fufufakin
nomine maferis fefeines spiritus amefies

(Norway, 19th century)

TALISMAN, WAX, AND RIVER WATER TO NAME A THIEF

To see who stole, write these words three times on paper and let it dry.

Take some white wax, as large as a pea, and use it to fasten the corners
of the paper in the bottom of a bowl. Get water from a running river or
a stream and fill the bowl. Hide the bowl for three nights in a secret
place. Then go to it again and you will see the name of the thief, where
the stolen item has gone, and where it can be found again.

(Norway, 18th century)

Read more about Norse folk magic in this book:
"Trolldom: Spells and Methods" by Johannes Bjorn Gardback

CHINESE TAOIST FU CHARMS

Fu means "luck" and fu charms can be crafted of virtually any material. Ideographic paper fu charms —vertical yellow papers with red, black, or red-and-black block printing and/or hand-written calligraphy — were once made only by Chinese Taoist priests, but these days they are also by professional fulu practitioners who know the auspicious days on which to produce them, and the prayers and gestures that accompany their creation.

Each Taoist sect has its own style of fu charms, and some sects do not recognize the charms of others as legitimate. Some, for instance, believe that the handles of the brushes used to write the charms should be of Peachwood only, that clients should submit hair or fingernail clippings to the fulu, and that each charm must bear the name and birth date of the client, while others freely transmit fu charms via books, by fax, and on the internet.

Some fu charms are culture-specific to Chinese Taoism: They summon named ghosts and spirits, exorcise evil entities, or invoke the assistance of deities such as Yu Huang Da Di The Jade Emperor, Jiu Tian Xuan Nu The Mysterious Lady of the Ninth Heaven, Lei Gong The Thunder God, Men Shen The Door Gods, and Ba Xian The Eight Immortals. Others are designed to assist in human affairs. They may help one to succeed in business, win the lottery, find a suitable mate, restore marital harmony, curse an enemy, protect a household, attract prosperity, negate attacks by sorcery, prevent burglary, or raise an obedient and intelligent child.

Fu charms may be hung up in the home or business or carried on the person. Additionally, because Taoism embraces Chinese traditional medicine, special fu charms to prevent miscarriage, stop bleeding, bring down fevers, ease toothache, or dissolve a bone lodged in the throat may be burned to ash and given to a patient to drink in a liquid.

CHINESE JOSS PAPER AND SPIRIT MONEY

A strong feature of Chinese folk religion is the veneration of ancestors through the burning of spirit money. Printed in imitation of real bank notes, and often imprinted as Hell Bank Notes or Heaven Bank Notes, these papers are burned to send financial assistance to ancestors in the afterworld. In some regions, the term joss paper (derived from the Portuguese word dios or god) is used to identify non-currency forms of spirit-money, including that which is overlaid with silver or fold foil or is printed in the form of daisy-like wheels.

Three Taoist fu charms written on paper, 1995 - 2015. The style of calligraphy utilized by practitioners varies greatly among the different schools of Taoist sorcery. The intentions of fu charms vary just as much as the calligraphy, and individual charms may be crafted as petitions for health, protection, money-getting, career, and scholarly excellence of children. Although paper fu charms come out of ancient traditions of magical calligraphy, they are now widely downloaded from the internet.

TAWEEZ: AN AFRICAN ARABIC CHARM IN AMERICA

A taweez or twiz is an Arabic amulet or talisman. One group of these consists of charms written on paper. Traditionally, taweez charms may be based in the text of a Surah or chapter of the Quran associated with a particular type of help or hope, and they may also contain a dua or plea for God's help. Taweez charms inscribed on metal may be worn as pendants, but those written on paper are generally folded repeatedly and deployed in a particular location or sewn into tiny cloth or leather pouches to wear.

The taweez shown here is both typical of the African style of working, and unusual because it is an Arabic charm made by a Ghanaian Muslim magician living in the U.S.A. He crafted it in 2006 for a Christian African-American client who is a customer of our hoodoo candle shop. It was sealed and she did not look inside. She was told to place it under a rock for protection. Eventually she retrieved it, undid the seals, opened the paper, and contacted us to see if we could find out what it said and meant. In 2012, my colleague ConjureMan Ali, who is fluent in Arabic, translated it:

"The outer boundary contains words of power that erect a barrier to bind and drive out evil djinn. It employs verses from Surah Ikhlas of the Quran, but the words are obfuscated by changing word order and letters, and omitting words; these are common techniques in taweez-making.

"The outer boundary of the talisman creates a symbolic protection around the inside boxes. Surah Ikhlas is commonly used to bind djinn and for protection. It itself is called the Key of the Quran as it contains within its four verses the entirety of the theology of Islam and the nature of God.

"Each corner of the talisman has the world *Bism* which means *In the Name* and is the beginning of another phrase of power written out in entirety at the top separate from the talisman: *Bismillahi rahman i rahim,* which means *In the Name of God the Most Merciful and Gracious.*

"The use of *Bism* or any other word to form the lines of the outer square is a very typical North African technique in taweez-making.

"What is written in the center of the talisman is too small to see, but it is likely the petition or prayer tied to the talisman. It would contain a name, lineage, and possible directions for the spirits tied to the talisman. I do note there is some mirror writing in it."

Read ConjureMan Ali's full description of this taweez online:
LuckyMojo.com/amulet-translate.html

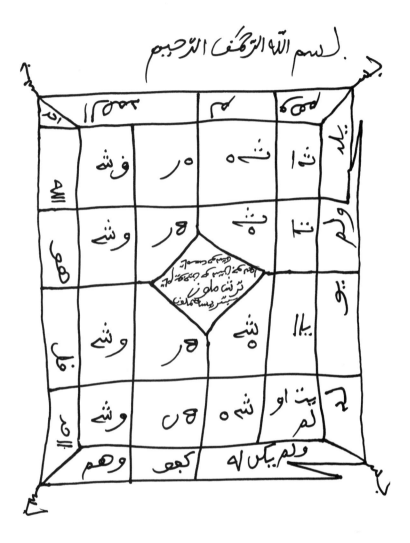

An Arabic taweez charm in the Ghanaian tradition, made in the United States for an African-American Christian client in 2006. Folded, sealed, and buried underneath a rock, it offers protection from evil spirits to the one for whom it was made. It employs verses from Surah Ikhlas (#112, the Surah of Purity and Sincerity) which begins, *"Say: He is Allah, the One!"*

THE *RI O* COMES TO HARLEM

Lurking behind the facade of the 1940s hoodoo author "Henri Gamache" is the odd fact that, according to her publisher's son, Ed Kay, she was a "young college-educated Jewish woman" living in New York City. Textual analysis of the "Gamache" corpus, including *The Master Book of Candle Burning, The Magic of Herbs, The Master Book of Occult Secrets, Terrors of the Evil Eye Exposed,* and *The Mystery of the Long Lost 8th, 9th, and 10th Books of Moses,* bears out Kay's remembrance. "Gamache" affixed scholarly bibliographies to her books, referred to Jewish rabbis, and cited academic German tomes. My own original copyright research reveals that her name was Anne Fleitman. She either worked with one Henry March (Henri Gamache) or used that as a secondary pseudonym.

Moses is the attributed author of the Pentateuch or first five books of the Bible. *The Sixth and Seventh Books of Moses* was an 18th century Jewish grimoire. Building upon the latter's already-extant popularity among hoodoo workers, Gamache's 1948 book, *The Mystery of the Long Lost 8th, 9th, and 10th Books of Moses,* gave conjure a transfusion of classical magic.

Gamache wrote that the Eighth Book of Moses is the *Leyden Papyrus,* found in Thebes in the 19th century, part of the collection dispersed by Jean d'Anastasi and translated in the *PGM.* Another manuscript included in her book is the 13th century *Sword of Moses,* written in Syrian Rabbinical Hebrew and Aramaic, which was translated into German by Moses Gaster.

The Bible tells us that Moses married a Cushite or Ethiopian woman, and Gamache promoted the Jamaican Marcus Garvey's belief that Moses himself was Black, a belief shared by many American Jews. She wrote that "Moses was born in Egypt," that "the religious practices of natives of the West Coast of Africa [trace] directly back to Egypt," that "these customs and religious beliefs came with the first slaves and ... grew up in the West Indies and in the Southern part of the United States," and that "the influence of Moses was not something which developed after [slaves] were brought to this new land." Her Afrocentric, classical, and kabbalist viewpoint has influenced four generations of Black Christian conjure and obeah workers.

Read more about Moses, the *PGM* and Afrocentric Judaism in this book:
"The Mystery of the Long Lost 8th, 9th, and 10th Books of Moses" by Henri Gamache
Read about Anne Flietman, Henry Marsh, and "Henri Gamache" here:
LuckyMojo.com/young.html

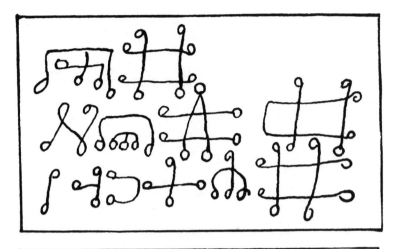

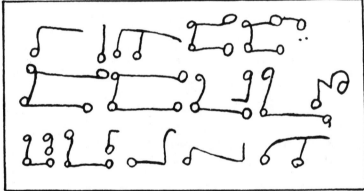

From *The Mystery of the Long Lost 8th, 9th, and 10th Books of Moses:*

At top is "A Seal So That the Devil Shall Smite an Enemy." The instructions are to "Take a stone and throw it to a Dog which shall bite it, and on it write these names and throw it in the house of thine enemy and thou shalt see wonders." Presumably the Devil will appear and you can watch the fun.

At bottom is "A Seal to Wreak Vengeance Upon an Enemy." The directions are to "Take this seal and wash it with water until it is clean and taking the water thereof and sprinkle it in the house of the enemy on the second night of the week or on the fourth of the week at the seventh hour."

ADOPTION AND ADAPTATION

While always keeping its inherent African character, Black American conjure culture has incorporated quite a few magical concepts and ways of working from geographic regions and religious lineages not generally associated with Africa. When such borrowings enter hoodoo, they either are retained verbatim or overlaid with African methodologies, giving them what anthropologists call a "creolized" form. This is as true of spell-papers and written charms of hoodoo as it is in Black music, art, and literature.

In conjure we see magical writings placed into containers, just as in ancient Egypt and Isræl — only instead of demon bowls we see sugar bowls and instead of phylacteries we see mojo bags.

Just as in ancient Greece and North Africa, written spells are deployed in graveyards — but they are also buried at crossroads.

Just as in old Scandinavia or Germany, written spells are worked at the threshold — but they are also placed under hearth bricks. And, of course, they are pinned to clothing or placed under a mattress.

In the True Length we were introduced to the magical use of the footprint of the Blessed Virgin. How like our "Paper in My Shoe" this is — and, in fact, foot-track magic is found throughout Europe, although there it forms a minor current of interest, not the large focus of practice that it does in Africa and among African-Americans.

In the Solomonic and Mosaic seals we see wholesale adoption of essentially Jewish kabbalistic work by Black rootworkers, especially the professionals who purchased curios and supplies by mail-order after 1900.

We see that the Arabic Taweez made by the Ghanian immigrant was purchased for use by a Black American woman who identified herself as both a Christian and a practitioner of hoodoo, but was willing to try what magic could come her way from the old African homeland.

Chinese joss paper and fu charms have also become popular among Black practitioners, especially those living in close proximity to Asians.

Having taken a ramble through history, we can now better recognize how hoodoo conjure doctors have adapted and adopted older elements of folk magic to make it their own. Having rambled around the world, we now have a better perspective on the culturally exotic sources from which Black practitioners have drawn and can draw their ideas. In the pages to follow, you will see both purely African and joyously creolized ways of working. Enjoy them both, for they are the warp and weft of the weave.

PUTTING PEN TO PAPER

At this point i need to explain a little bit about why this book exists. Back in 2002, when i wrote *Hoodoo Herb and Root Magic*, i only expected it to reach the audience from which the material had come in the first place, that is, African-American practitioners. I figured there was no need to tell folks how to write a paper because they already knew how, and all they would want would be my convenient lists of herbs and roots. However, for better or worse (and i think it was a bit of both, actually) that book took off flying. It introduced a whole lot of people to hoodoo who had never heard of it before. They didn't know the basics of the work. They didn't know how to write a name paper. They didn't know what a petition was. They had no Black friends, so they couldn't ask for help.

The thing is, i had put several examples of papers into the herb book, but the only reason they were there was because they were unusual. They were the oddball papers. They were the ones so different than the norm that i thought them worth documenting. I figured everyone already knew how to write ten types of "regular" papers, and part of what i was doing was just showing off my typesetting skills, so it never occurred to me that people would take those examples as some kind of gospel or "rule." But they did.

For the next ten years i kept hearing folks say things like, "You have to write the name an odd number of times and write your wish in a circle around it because that's how it's done in hoodoo." It kinda freaked me out.

I knew things had gone too far when an older Southern Black women, not quite my age, said, "I don't know if i'm writing my papers out right. My mother always told me to write them one right over the other, but in your book, you show them criss-cross." I couldn't believe it. This nice woman was about to give up a great old-school way of working because she had seen a different way in a book — my book! I told her, "No, wait up there, your way is right! Your mother was right. Your way is just fine!"

But as we kept on talking, i realized that by publishing those few oddball papers, without describing the basic, time tested, usual ways, i had inadvertently allowed distortion and malformation to creep into the very practice i sought to preserve. I knew i had to rectify my error.

So that's where we are right now. This book exists to rectify my error. It's time to go back to basics. It's time to start with the simplest of techniques, putting pen to paper.

WHAT TO WRITE UPON

ORDINARY PAPERS AND SPECIAL PAPERS

In hoodoo, the most common writing surface is paper. We do not write on lead sheets like the ancient Greeks (not available) or on wooden staves like the Scandinavians (we never got into runes). We rarely use animal skin parchment or vellum (too expensive), but we often use parchment paper (easy to find and reasonably priced). We may use fancy gilded Asian spirit money (if we live near Asian people). We may think a 3" square Post-It note is cool (if we can work the stickiness in our favour). But when it comes down to it, we most likely will use lined composition paper, unlined copy paper, fine-grain shopping bag paper, or coarse-grain grocery sack paper, neatly torn on all four sides to make a square or a triangle.

WORDS ON WAX

In addition to writing on paper, we can inscribe free-standing candles. I use a pin, a needle, a nail, or a small pen-knife for this task. Some call it "carving" the candle, but i don't. To me "carving" means using a sharp-ended, wood-handled tool to craft an image out of a cylindrical candle. That is "carving." But when we write in wax, all we are doing is inscribing, so let's call it that. No, the candle is not a paper — but the writing on it sure is writing. Remember that just as we bathe upward to draw or downward to clean, we can apply directionality to candle inscription. The best method is to spiral the petition up or down the candle, like stripes on a barber pole.

HAVE YOU EVER WRITTEN ON A PLATE?

When i was young, i used to watch the Spiritual Church ladies write on white plates. Why? Well, to wash them off, of course. The water that washes off words contains those words. It is powerfully imbued with what those words stand for, and you can use it in cooking, cleaning, or baths.

WRITING ON MONEY

We prepare currency with written names, wishes, scripture, glyphs, or sigils. Common methods include signing a name under the Treasurer's name, adding the $$¢¢$$ sigil for trained hunting money, or marking bills with RTM for "Return To Me." We may also inscribe coins.

HANDWRITING SAMPLES

A piece of paper that someone wrote on is a combination writing surface and personal concern. Write your command on it! If you can't get a person's handwriting, why not? Proximity makes for effective magic.

CHECKS, BUSINESS CARDS, AND LOGOS

If you are working on spells regarding businesses or bosses, if you face a court case, if you are applying for a job, or if you are trying to get a loan, write on a piece of paper connected to the enterprise at hand. Ask for or take business cards, print corporate logos off the internet, save notes that were handed to you at work. These are personal concerns as well as papers.

PLAYING CARDS

Professor Charles Porterfield advises us on playing cards as papers: "The names of clients or targets are easily written onto the heads or feet of the appropriate royal cards with a Sharpie. Add in a birth date and a simple command, and these cards quickly become effective and stylistic name papers. If the card was touched by the target, so much the better, as it becomes a personal concern as well as a symbolic proxy of the person."

ALUMINUM FOIL, PIE PLATES, AND POPSICLE STICKS

Remember those Greco-Roman defixiones and Swedish runkafles? Bet you never thought that style of working would be so modern and up-to-date, did you? Two words, folks: *Aluminum Foil*. Before you wrap a freezer spell in foil, use a soft pencil to impress commands all over the foil. And you know those cheap, disposable aluminum pie plates? You probably already use them for burning candles, or you ought to, so now you know to write on them before you set the lights. And don't forget the popsicle stick that someone licked: Write the person's name and your command on it!

PHOTOGRAPHS

Photographs have been around since the mid-19th century. My oldest ancestor who lived long enough to have his photo taken was born in 1794. That's old! But people still sometimes balk at using a photo as a name paper. They seem to think it's not "authentic." Oh, yes it is — and what's more, with the development of digital technology, you never have to ruin a relic. Just scan that photo and you can print another copy later.

WHAT TO WRITE WITH

STYLUS

A stylus is a writing tool that leaves marks but does not emit ink or graphite. We use ready-to-hand tools for this task, including pins, needles, nails, and knife-points to inscribe candles or wax figures, or to mark a petition on aluminum foil, pie plates, or the cups that tea-lights come in. A worn-out soft-lead pencil can also be used as a stylus on aluminum.

QUILL, DIP-PEN, AND FOUNTAIN PEN

Bird feather quill-pens, metal-nibbed dip pens, and fountain pens are now obsolete but continue in use because they allow the practitioner to work with specially prepared inks. Dyed quills are colour-coded: white for healing, blessing, and protection; red for love and sex; green for money and luck; and black for reversing, revenge, and crossing.

PENCIL

Pencils come in two types, those with erasers and those that were made without erasers. A wise old woman once told me to write petitions with pencils that were made without erasers, "so you can't go back on your word." That resonated with me, and i have been using church pew pencils ever since. It's not a "rule." I just like the way they look and feel.

BALLPOINT PEN, ROLLERBALL PEN, AND MARKER

Any style of modern pen can be used to write a petition. You can select them by colour (red for love is a common choice) or by base (water-based to wash into water, permanent for use out-of-doors) or just go with what you've got. If you are writing on laminated playing cards, try a Sharpie.

MAGICAL INKS

The three old-school European magical inks — Dove's Blood, Bat's Blood, and Dragon's Blood — are still manufactured, for those who use feather quills. Some old spells ask for petitions written in blood, but frankly, you will see that sort of stuff more often in the movies than in real rootwork.

OTHER STATIONERY SUPPLIES

Be sure to have scissors, tape, and glue on hand. You'll need them.

HOW TO FOLD A PAPER

Let's start simple. You don't have to fold a paper. All you have to do is put it under a candle or in your shoe and you are practicing conjure.

Shoe papers go face-up, but with candle-papers you have a choice. If your petition is for good things, lay the paper face-up. If your desires are coercive, place it face-down, because you want to keep work like that private and confidential. You can put the paper under a plate and set the candle stand on the plate. An inscribed aluminum pie pan is also discreet.

If you are working an apple or onion spell, roll the paper into a tube. If you are accordion-folding paper to reduce an enemy's stature, do just that. Crumple a paper into a ball to push it in a bottle or to make a pill to swallow.

Most other forms of folding follow a simple plan. You fold the paper away from you to remove things or people, and you fold it toward you to bring in things or people. You can fold repeatedly to make a small packet, but don't expect that it will securely hold the ingredients that you put into it. To keep them tidy, you will need to fold your paper seed-packet style.

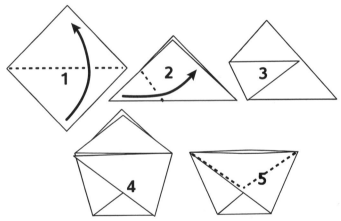

Here's how to make a seed-packet out of a 3-inch square Post-It note:
1. After you write on the paper, fold it in half on the diagonal.
2. Fold the left corner up so that its top is parallel to the bottom edge.
3. Fold the right corner up to the left, also parallel to the bottom edge.
4. Fill the envelope with herbs, powders, curios, or personal concerns.
5. Fold the two free tips into the pocket formed by the outside flap.

WHAT'S IN A PRAYER?

IMPROVISATION FROM SCRIPTURE

Throughout this book you will find scriptural prayers cited by chapter and verse, so that you can look them up. Additionally, i have told you to write prayers in your own words, from the heart. If you were brought up in church, you won't need schooling. If not, please look over this exemplary petition paper. It was turned in as homework by Donnice Rome, a graduate of my Hoodoo Rootwork Correspondence Course. If you just fell into hoodoo because you think it's "witchy," you may be wondering why she wrote what she did. But if you know your Bible, you can almost sing along:

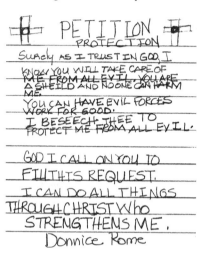

Isaiah 12:2: *"Surely God is my salvation; I will trust and not be afraid."*
Jeremiah 40:4: *"Come, and I will take care of you."*
Psalms 91: *"His truth shall be thy shield and buckler."*
Psalms 140:4: *"Protect me, Lord, from the control of evil people."*
Philippians 4:13*: "I can do all things through Christ who strengthens me."*

PRAYER REQUEST AND PSALMS 66:19 ON A PAPER

This way of affirming a prayer comes out of the Spiritual Churches, where it is used in candle services. You may also work this way at home. Write your prayer or wish on one side of a narrow slip of paper, and speak it out loud. On the other side of the slip of paper, write out Psalms 66:19: *"Verily God hath heard me; he hath attended to the voice of my prayer."* Wrap the slip of paper, Psalm side outward, around the base of an offertory candle of a colour appropriate to your request, and glue the paper to itself to form a continuous band. Stick the candle into a pan of clean sand and burn it through in one setting.

WHAT'S IN A PETITION?

WORDS OF POWER

Formulating a concise and pithy petition requires artistry. My personal æsthetics (and perhaps an ancestral call to Jewish microcalligraphy) have led me to spend hours crafting and perfecting petitions, not because they are "more effective" if well made, but just because i like the work. I favour short phrases in grids, circles, or squares. I also enjoy typesetting. But those are my own ways. You are not obliged to copy me or ape my style.

In the 1960s, i was told by a couple of folks to "write your command in one continuous line, without picking up your pencil to dot your i's or cross your t's until the words join up again." I became hooked on the intensity of focus it took to accomplish this simple task. Never mind that most of my teachers never mentioned such a strenuous exercise of will at all — i loved the challenge, and i rose to it. You do not have to. Really, you do not. God will be able to read your petition if you misspell every word. And if radial or four-fold symmetry is not your thing, just write. Just write out what you want and what you mean to get:

With all the power of my strong right hand, i smite and crush
The man who took my books in trade and gave me nothing in return!
May he die like the dog he is, and with him all his lies and infamy!
May he go down to his grave of raging drink and drugs unmourned,
And join the vile J. H. who ate my food and stole my texts. Amen!

Four examples of petition papers typeset by the author, 2002 and 2015:
Top: A genuine curse of death upon two thieves, and they know who they are.
Left: "Faithful to a Trust," a rock-strong, four-square wall of polite command.
Middle: "lovelovelovelovelove," a rolling wheel of harmonic sexual bliss.
Right: "Love Me or Die," the worst imaginable form of graveyard love.

WHAT'S IN A NAME?

VARIATIONS ON A SINGLE NAME
Here is a straight name paper, written out one time:

John Russell Brown

Here is the same name with a birth date added:

John Russell Brown, July 4th, 1949

Here is the name with the birth date rendered as a line of numbers:

John Russell Brown
7 . 4 . 1949

Here the person's name, birth date, and zodiac sign are combined:

John Russell Brown July 4th, 1949

Here is the name written out one time, plus some glyphic commentary:

Here the person's middle name is replaced with words of power:

John DEATH Brown   **John LOVE Brown**   **John JUSTICE Brown**

Here the person's name has been written out multiple times:

John Russell Brown
John Russell Brown
John Russell Brown

Here is the name written out in block capitals one time, with glyphs between each letter. These are crosses, for a blessing:

J + O + H + N + R + U + S + S + E + L + L + B + R + O + W + N

The name and the glyphs may be written out multiple times, just as would be done for a plain name:

J + O + H + N + R + U + S + S + E + L + L + B + R + O + W + N
J + O + H + N + R + U + S + S + E + L + L + B + R + O + W + N
J + O + H + N + R + U + S + S + E + L + L + B + R + O + W + N
J + O + H + N + R + U + S + S + E + L + L + B + R + O + W + N
J + O + H + N + R + U + S + S + E + L + L + B + R + O + W + N
J + O + H + N + R + U + S + S + E + L + L + B + R + O + W + N
J + O + H + N + R + U + S + S + E + L + L + B + R + O + W + N

The letters and glyphs may written in checkerboard form to fill an entire square of paper:

```
J + O + H + N + B + R + O + W + N +
+ J + O + H + N + B + R + O + W + N
J + O + H + N + B + R + O + W + N +
+ J + O + H + N + B + R + O + W + N
J + O + H + N + B + R + O + W + N +
+ J + O + H + N + B + R + O + W + N
J + O + H + N + B + R + O + W + N +
+ J + O + H + N + B + R + O + W + N
J + O + H + N + B + R + O + W + N +
+ J + O + H + N + B + R + O + W + N
J + O + H + N + B + R + O + W + N +
+ J + O + H + N + B + R + O + W + N
J + O + H + N + B + R + O + W + N +
+ J + O + H + N + B + R + O + W + N
J + O + H + N + B + R + O + W + N +
+ J + O + H + N + B + R + O + W + N
J + O + H + N + B + R + O + W + N +
+ J + O + H + N + B + R + O + W + N
```

The letters and glyphs may be neatly stacked and centered:

$$+ J + O + H + N +$$
$$+ R + U + S + S + E + L + L +$$
$$+ B + R + O + W + N +$$

You may use glyphic dollar signs for a money spell:

J $ O $ H $ N $ R $ U $ S $ S $ E $ L $ L $ B $ R $ O $ W $ N

Here the success sigil replaces the person's middle name:

John $$¢¢$$ Brown

Here is the name written in script with glyphic heart signs for a love spell:

♥ ♥ ♥ *John Russell Brown* ♥ ♥ ♥

Here the name is written in block capitals with heart signs for love; alternatively, the hearts may be outlines with a letter inside each heart:

♥ J ♥ O ♥ H ♥ N ♥
♥ R ♥ U ♥ S ♥ S ♥ E ♥ L ♥ L ♥
♥ B ♥ R ♥ O ♥ W ♥ N ♥

Here is the name written out in block capitals with an eye glyph between each letter. These eyes may be used to symbolize watchful awareness of an enemy or protection from the evil eye:

👁 J 👁 O 👁 H 👁 N 👁
👁 R 👁 U 👁 S 👁 S 👁 E 👁 L 👁 L 👁
👁 B 👁 R 👁 O 👁 W 👁 N 👁

WHAT'S IN TWO NAMES?

VARIATIONS ON MULTIPLE NAMES

Here are two names side by side, as equals:

John Russell Brown   Abigail Samantha Little

Here are two names written right on top of one another. The top one rules and controls the other:

Abigail Samantha Little

Here are two names crossed like a Christian cross:

Here is a name written three times. The paper was rotated 90 degrees (some folks say "clockwise to move things forward and counterclockwise to remove them," but others only say, "turn the paper a quarter-turn"). The second name is written three times, to form a grid. This is called crossing and covering. You can also cross the names in an X or make a grid seven by seven or nine by nine, or cross one name over 34 names to rule them all! There is no one way to criss-cross names.

Here two names are running into each other to bring about a meeting.

John Russell Brown ɘltti⅃ ɒrtnɒmɒƧ liɒpidA

Here two names are running away from one another. This is done to separate people, and when inscribing double action candles to return evil to the sender:

nwoɿ⺙ llɘƨƨuЯ nrloↃ Abigail Samantha Little

Here are two names written back to back and not touching, ready to be cut apart for a Break Up spell:

Clareesa Tremaine

And, finally, you can write three names in an equilateral triangle if your goal is equality among three business partners or in a triadic relationship.

IS REPETITION NECESSARY?

HOW MANY TIMES SHOULD YOU WRITE THE NAME?

Next comes a topic that i have very strong opinions about:
How many times should you write out a name on a name paper?
My firm belief is that there is no one answer to this question. It depends on what you wish to accomplish, the kind and size of paper you have, where you will be putting that paper, and whether anything will be written on the paper in addition to the name. Sure, some folks who have been in this work for a long time do have favourite numbers — three, seven, and nine are often cited — and they instruct those whom they teach to repeat a name their favourite number of times, almost every time they teach:

"Write his name nine times on a sheet of virgin parchment."

"Write the boss's name three times on the back of his business card."

"Write his name seven times, then turn the paper 90 degrees clockwise and write your name seven times to cross and cover his."

"Write his name twice, diagonally from corner to corner on the back of the business card, like an X."

Those are indeed common instructions, but just as common, and not specifically counted, are these instructions:

"Write his name over and over and over on both sides of the paper, down one side and up the other, very neatly, in rows."

"Write his name as many times as he is years old."

"Write out the entire Psalm with his initials in place of each verse number in the Psalm."

Not only do certain practitioners have favourite numbers, there are also certain ways of working that more or less lead the practitioner to prescribe a certain number of repetitions. For instance, if a worker likes square rather than rectangular papers, repeating the name an odd number of times to form a block will become habit. On the other hand, if the worker makes tiny little tobies, the notion of writing the name only one time will assert itself, because you can't write a name seven times on a paper small enough to seal into a silver locket. In a case like that, you may hear the worker say:

"I want you to write your name one time, really small, on a slip of paper no larger than the kind of paper that comes in a Chinese fortune cookie."

The truth is, some spells will be told with specific numbers cited, and others will not. Sometimes the choice is yours. Get used to it!

BUT I DON'T KNOW THE NAME!

IF YOU DON'T KNOW THE NAME, HERE'S WHAT TO DO
Although it is not a bodily concern like toenails, hair, or semen, a name paper is still a proxy for a person. It can be boiled, stabbed, burned, kissed, anointed, stepped on, or loved. As you do unto it, you do unto that person.

So, if a name paper is such a powerful link to a person — what if you don't know the name? Can you still do the work? Will it succeed?

If you do not know the person's name, but you do know the person's location, you will have to get creative in your design of the name paper.

The simplest way is to describe the person and write out the address where the person lives or where you see the person:

> *The cute, short Chinese girl*
> *who waits for the bus every morning*
> *at Sacramento Street and University Avenue*

This descriptive paper will not be as strong a link to "the Chinese girl" as a name paper would be, but it will do to get you started. Once you learn her name, you can either add it to that paper or start a new paper on her.

The same sort of generalized description is useful if you are writing out a collective name paper for a group of people:

> *The Creepy Methamphetamine Addicts at*
> *3456 Ardmore Boulevard, Apartment B.*

Note that even though you don't know the names of the drug addicts, their descriptive paper is a better link than the one for the girl at the bus stop, because it contains their home address, not just a public street corner.

Another way to work if you don't know someone's name is to take a photo with your cell phone. Be discreet if you do this, of course.

If you are working on something to do with a place of business or a corporation, get the company's logo from the internet, print it out, and use it as a name paper. If you can go into the business and legitimately ask for or pick up a business card, that is even better, because someone in the company touched it when it was put into the business card holder.

NO NAME, NO BIRTH DATE, NO ADDRESS. NOW WHAT?

When a brand new client asks me to put a death spell on someone but she has no name, no birth date, and no address for her enemy, i question her closely. Is she really sure there actually is an enemy — or did some unscrupulous fake worker convince her that she is "under attack"?

My next question is if this other worker convinced my new client that there is an enemy on her tail, then why didn't the client stick with the other worker and get the matter taken care of there? So i ask that question.

The answer will almost always be that the other worker wanted multi-thousands of dollars to take off the attack by the unidentified "enemy" and the client didn't have the money, so she came to me because i am cheaper. So i do a check-reading.

Sometimes, if my reading reveals no attack or curse is underway, i have a very angry new client to deal with, because, hey, she just paid $12,000 to some scam worker and i am flat-out telling her that she was scammed.

But let's say that my reading agrees with the previous one. She is cursed. And i can't see who did it. What does she do now?

I tell her to write out whatever she does know, like so:

MY ENEMY

MY WOMAN'S OTHER MAN

THAT ROMANIAN WHORE

THE GUY WHO STOLE MY BIKE

After that, she can write her command on top of or across the name:

DIE A MISERABLE, PAINFUL DEATH, YOU GOD FORSAKEN MOTHER FUCKER

FIND YOUR OWN NO-GOOD MAN AND LEAVE MY NO-GOOD MAN ALONE

This same technique is useful for the person who has found evidence that his or her mate is cheating, but doesn't know with whom.

GLYPHS AND FLOWERS

BE CREATIVE IN YOUR CORNERS
The corners of a petition paper are where you can get creative. God's watchful eye, a decorative border of flowers, four hearts, flames of love (or flames of anger), or four houses, each with a stylized path that leads to the next house — all of these add individuality to your work.

PAPER TRICKS

SEWING OR PINNING PAPERS TOGETHER
To keep a couple together, fix their names or photos face-to-face. Cross two needles in an X, use a safety pin, or sew them with a binding stitch.

TEARING A PAPER BAG
If you have no lined paper or fancy parchment, write on a unprinted kraft paper sack that has been neatly torn on all four sides. One woman showed me how to do this in her shop, explaining that, "If there is no machine-cut edge, then that paper will be so pure that the angels could read it or write on it."

COLOUR-CODED PAPERS
A woman told me that a worker she knew before World War Two colour-coded her petition papers: A baby was rice-paper, a Caucasian was white paper, a Hispanic was newsprint, a light-skinned Negro was a light brown stationery bag, and a dark skinned Negro was a dark brown grocery bag. This paralleled her using different types of sugar (powdered, granulated, light brown, and dark brown) to symbolize the people she was sweetening.

TRIANGULAR CURSES
I have been told many times to scissor-cut paper into an acute triangle when writing out a curse, to "make it sharp-cornered and hurt them."

A HEART, A SNOWFLAKE, A CHAIN OF PAPER DOLLS
Remember the patterns you cut out of construction paper when you were young? Of course you do. The Valentine's heart-shaped paper is for love, the Christmas snowflake is for family holidays, and the happy chain of paper dolls is for all the ladies in the office — name them, every one!

TAKING A MEASURE

THE MEASURE IS A PERSONAL CONCERN

Quite a few conjure spells employ the "measure" of some part of the person's body. The most common measures are the genitals and the foot. The measure of the genitals is referred to euphemistically as "the measure of a man" or "the measure of a woman," but it is not the same as the "true length" of the man or woman, which runs from head to foot. The measure of the foot is always specified as "of the foot" and should not be confused with the measure of a man or the measure of a woman. Other measures may be taken as well, as described below.

The measure may be captured or marked on a string, a piece of cloth, or a piece of paper. It may be imbued with the person's bodily fluids, particularly sexual fluids or foot sweat. It may be transferred from one system of marking to another, for instance from a string to a piece of paper or from a visual mark on the hand to a string. After it is captured, it will be used in a spell. If it is captured on paper, the paper may also be written upon with a name, petition, prayer, or visual designs.

THE MEASURE OF A MAN

There are two entirely different ways to take the measure of a man. Both have been described with such admirable specificity that it is impossible to think that they are the same, but although some workers prefer one method over another and will only use their favoured method, both techniques are traditional among Black practitioners of the past and the present, and neither is "better" than the other.

One way is to measure around the erect penis. This is done by encircling the member with the thumb and forefinger and noting where the joints overlap, then uncurling the fingers and marking the resultant length on a paper. This is sometimes called the "width" of the member. It is most commonly used in spells involving fidelity.

The other, and more common method, is to measure the erect penis along your hand by putting the tip of the middle finger at the man's groin and mentally noting how far his penis reaches onto your hand or wrist. This visual mark is then transferred to a string or piece of paper. The paper may include a graphic representation of the sex organ. This type of measure may be used in any kind of sex, love, fidelity, or fertility spell.

THE MEASURE OF A WOMAN

The measure of a woman is only taken in one way, as far as i know: It runs the length of the perineum from clitoris to anus. To take the measure, place the tip of the middle finger (or the thumb) on the clitoris and note how far down the hand the anus is. This is transferred to a string or a piece of paper. The paper may include a graphic representation of the sex organs; it may be used in any sort of sex, love, fidelity, or fertility spell.

THE MEASURE OF A FOOT

The measure of the foot is made either by marking the length of a person's foot-track in dirt or sand or by measuring the insole of a shoe that has been worn long enough to conform to the shape of the person's foot. The insole from a discarded shoe may be used as a measure. Additionally, in some spells, an actual tracing of the foot may be made with the cooperation of the person for whom the work is being done.

The use of foot-track dirt is so prevalent in conjure that if you see a foot-track in dirt or sand you should not only take the measure, but capture the actual track itself. Many magical uses for foot-track dirt are outside the scope of this book, but you will find them described in other spell-books.

THE MEASURE OF A HAND

Hand tracings on paper have a small but distinct place in rootwork and a couple of spells that use them are mentioned in this book.

CAPTURING A TRUE LENGTH OR A SHADOW

The true length may be captured by observing the person as he or she lays down, either in a bed or outdoors on the grass or a sandy beach. Visually note the position of the person's head and feet, and once he or she gets up and leaves, lay a string along the length and knot it at head and foot to preserve the measure. A true length may be transferred to paper if desired. If the person lay in sand or on dirt, it is considered very wise to capture some of that sand or dirt.

A child's true length is easily gotten by making growth marks in a doorframe. Adults can be cajoled into being marked in this way as a comparison to the child, and thus will record their true lengths unawares.

To capture a shadow, observe where the person stands and trace or mark the dimensions of the shadow, with or without the person's knowledge.

BURNING PAPERS TO ASH

THE POWER OF ASHES

There are a number of traditional spiritual uses for ashes in hoodoo, and they seem to be used in ways that speak to an African origin.

In Africa, magicians of many tribes use ashes as a form of concentrated spiritual marker (a "personal concern" or "magical link") to convey the essence of a plant, place, thing, or person into a spell, rite, trick, or spiritual supply. You can read about the use of ash in anthropological books on African sorcery and witchcraft of the 19th and 20th centuries, such as *Witchcraft, Oracles and Magic Among the Azande* by E. E. Evans-Pritchard (Oxford, 1937). You can also research the use of ashes in the mooyoo or magical "load" of the nkisi figures of Gabon and adjacent regions.

These African ways of working with ashes have survived in hoodoo. For instance, during the 1930s, Harry Hyatt recorded a spell from an informant in which the name of a person was burned to ash and used to represent the person in making a compound to be laid on the ground for foot-track magic. During the 1960s and 1970s i too learned many such ways of working with the ashes of names, petitions, and portions of scripture.

PRAYER OR SCRIPTURAL VERSE ASH

Hand-writing a prayer, either in your own words, or using scriptural texts from the Bible, produces a heightened form of the prayer or text. When you take the time to write out a Psalm, a verse, or a chapter from the Bible, or to compose your own prayer, you are making a connection from your head to heart to hand. The prayer carries its own Jewish and Christian religious connotations and weight, but added to it is the thought you have spent composing the material or reciting it in your mind as you wrote out the paper, and the time your hands have spent conveying those conceptions to the paper.

A prayer paper of this sort can be soaked in water and the water drunk to cleanse the body, but another common way of working is to burn the paper to ashes and blend the ashes into the materials used in another spiritual job. You may burn the paper to ashes in the flame of a candle and let it float upward, but a useful method for those who want to concentrate their efforts is to burn the paper on a bed of incense, either resin incense on charcoal or self-lighting powder incense, or a mixture of the two.

HOW TO BURN PAPERS ON INCENSE

Burning a name paper, affirmation, petition, prayer paper, or written verse of scripture on incense means that the name or prayer becomes part of the incense, and the ash from the incense contains the prayers or the name. Incense ash is uniform in texture compared to plain paper ash, and such ash can be mixed with local dirt, graveyard dirt, sachet powders, powdered herbs, more incense, or sand.

Then, depending upon what the ash was mixed with and what you are working on, or what you intend the outcome of your work to be, the resulting ash mixture can be sprinkled around the property, cooked into food, mixed with sachet powders for use in drawing designs on the altar, or used to line incense burners or candle trays.

HOW TO MAKE BIBLE ASHES OF PSALMS 91

The technique of burning paper to ash is probably more often applied to Psalms 91 than to any other text. Here are some of the ways i have been told to prepare the ashes. These methods come out of the Spiritual Church Movement or were shared by workers acquainted with that tradition. All of the instructions refer to the text of the Psalm. These instructions were given to me in full or in part by several people in my youth.

To burn Psalms 91 to ashes:

You take the paper out of the middle of a pad of paper that has lain in a closed desk drawer *("He that dwelleth in the secret place")*.

You write it out by hand with a white Goose-quill pen *("He shall cover thee with his feathers, and under his wings shalt thou trust")*.

You look carefully at each word as you write and you should be alone in the room at the time. *("Only with thine eyes shalt thou behold")*.

You sign the Psalm with your own name, as a testimony *("Because he hath known my name")*.

You stand on the finished paper bare-footed or in your stocking feet *("Lest thou dash thy foot against a stone")*.

You pick up and hold the paper to your heart *("His truth shall be thy shield and buckler")*.

You hold up the finished paper on your two palms-up hands *("They shall bear thee up in their hands")*.

You burn the finished paper to ash on a surface higher than the surface on which you wrote it *("I will set him on high")*.

EXODUS ASHES FOR LINING INCENSE BURNERS

When preparing new incense burners for use, no matter what they are made from, they must be lined with some sort of insulating material to keep them from overheating. (Even metal incense burners will burn through if kept unlined.) The two most common linings are clean sand and clean ash. The following method combines these two liners with prayer.

Write out the portion of Exodus 30:1 that consists of the single line: *"And thou shalt make an altar to burn incense upon"*

Write this over and over on a small sheet of paper, one line after the other, on both sides of the piece of paper. The paper should be wide enough to contain the line of text without it flowing over to the next line, just as if you were being asked to copy a piece of text on a chalk board at school, each line the same as the one above.

The number of times you write this line is not important, just write it over and over from top to bottom until the paper is filled, then turn the paper over and fill the other side the same way, with the same text, from top to bottom.

Set the paper on fire in your new incense brazier and it will burn up quickly to black carbon ash. Slowly add some of your clean sand and rub or crush it into the prayer paper ashes, until they are blended into the sand. Rub around the entire inside of the incense burner, then shake it to settle the sand and ashes at the bottom, and it is ready to use as a base on which to burn charcoal disks and resin or self-lighting incense.

NAME PAPER ASH, WITH OR WITHOUT QUASSIA BARK

It is a well-known and often practiced way of working to triple-refine a name or "concentrate" it by burning it, folding the ash into a second name paper, burning that, and folding the ash into a third name paper. This is used when no personal concerns can be had, as a way of concentrating the name.

It is common to fold Quassia Bark chips into the name papers when burning them, that is, to burn the Quassia Bark with the name paper each time and to mix the name paper ash and Quassia Bark ash. Quassia Bark is the only herb i know that is routinely used in this way.

Back in the day when people wrote with fountain pens, sprinkling the ash of a name paper on the second and third written iterations was also practiced because the ash actually stuck to the liquid ink as it dried.

DISSOLVING YOUR PETITIONS

The custom of writing out prayers or magical spells, washing them off or dissolving them into a liquid, and then doing something with the liquid is old-school magic, the kind that people have been performing ever since writing was invented.

Depending on what you intend to do with the liquid, you may use water, tea, whiskey, wine, beer, soda pop, urine, Four Thieves Vinegar, Buffalo Ammonia, perfume, or a pan of scrub water. The purpose of the spell may help influence your choice of liquid, but if you think about your options for a minute, you will come up with so many ways to use dissolved prayers and petitions that you could fill this page all on your own.

The work is simplicity itself. All you have to do is to write your prayer or petition with soluble ink so that it will come off in the liquid you have selected. Pray and focus as you write, and pray again as you dip the paper into the liquid and watch the ink flow into solution.

If you are concerned about drinking inky water, use food colours or Beet juice to write. And remember, you need not write on paper. A glyph or short prayer written in Olive Oil on a white plate and washed into water carries the essence of the prayer, no matter if that water is used to infuse a magical tea, for cooking, in the bath, in the laundry, or as a floor wash.

Read more about magical bathing and house cleaning in this book:
"Hoodoo Spiritual Baths" by Aura Laforest

DISPOSING OF YOUR PAPERS

Unless you burned or packaged up your paper, it may be left behind after your spell is completed. You may find this useful if you want to save the paper or packet to use again, but if you don't want to save the paper, burning it and scattering the ashes is a nice final touch, as is burying it. If you dissolved a paper in liquid and your paper is weak but your liquid is strong, your paper may dissolved away to scraps. If your paper was strong and your liquid was innocuous, you can take the paper out, dry it, eat it, burn it to ashes, or bury it, as you will.

Read more about disposing of ritual remains online here:
LuckyMojo.com/layingtricks.html

BLESSING SPELLS

BACKACHE MASSAGE CURE WITH THE PSALMS

If you have a headache or a backache, write out Psalms 3 by hand on clean paper and burn the paper to ashes. Mix the ashes with Olive Oil or 7-11 Holy Oil and a few drops of Peppermint Oil, praying Psalms 3 as you stir it together. Use the oil to massage your temples or your back.

TO HELP OR HEAL SOMEONE DEAR TO YOU

Make a name paper for the person whom you wish to heal or help. Wrap a hair from the person, a slice of Peony Root, and a small cross in the paper and carry it in red flannel bag. The cross will ward off evil and break jinxes. The Peony Root brings health and long life, and is said to cure mental illness or substance abuse. Dress the bag with Protection, Blessing, Healing, Cast Off Evil, or Run Devil Run Oil, as you prefer.

FOR COURAGE AND BRAVERY

Write your fears on paper and cross them with your own name written nine times. On the back write out Psalms 27: 1 (*"The Lord is my light and my salvation; whom shall I fear? the Lord is the strength of my life; of whom shall I be afraid?"*) Carry the paper in a yellow bag with a pinch each of Yarrow and Nettle, and you will eventually overcome your fears.

THE GUARDIAN ANGEL PRAYER FOR A CHILD

To teach a child about spiritual matters and also provide protection for the child, obtain a copy of the Guardian Angel picture that depicts an angel watching over two children. Write out this prayer yourself and have the child sign it: *"Angel of God, my guardian dear / To whom His love commits me here / Ever this day be at my side / To light and guard, to rule and guide. / Amen."* Frame the picture and hang it over the child's bed.

TO INCREASE A WOMAN'S CHANCE OF CONCEPTION

Working from the bottom end, where the little hole is, inject a ripe fresh Fig full of honey, and insert into it a tightly rolled paper on which is written, *"Baby, child of [father], born from the womb of [mother]."* Place the filled Fig in a small jar of honey, stem-end up, seal the jar, and bury it in the yard or under the path where the woman will step over it.

MONEY AND LUCK SPELLS

WEALTHY WAY

On the back of a dollar bill, write this verse of Deuteronomy 28:8: *"The Lord shall command the blessing upon thee in thy storehouses, and in all that thou settest thine hand unto; and he shall bless thee in the land which the Lord thy God giveth thee."* On the front of the dollar bill write your first and last names. Place them under a plate.

Inscribe your name on a green offertory candle and dress it with Wealthy Way Oil. Burn it for a few minutes every evening when you come home from work. Drip oil on the wick each time you light it. After five days of work, you are ready for your weekend, so come home and put five drops of oil on the dollar bill — at the corners and center. Then light the money on fire and burn it to ashes. Rub the ashes on the soles of your shoes, let the candle burn to the socket, and go out and have a good time.

A MOJO FOR GETTING A LOAN TO BUY SOMETHING

Write your monetary petition *("Grant me the loan of $12,000.00")* or your affirmation *("The Bank of Umexa loans me $12,000.00")* or your prayer *("Dear Lord, Please sway the heart of Miss Sibley, the loan officer at the Bank of Umexa, that she may consent to loan me $12,000.00")* on a piece of paper and sign it with your name. On top of this, lay a small catalogue photo of whatever item you intend to purchase with the loan. On top of the photo place a pinch of Alfalfa leaves, a pinch of Five Finger Grass, and several whole Cloves. Wrap everything up into a packet and carry it in a green mojo bag dressed with Crown of Success Oil and Hoyt's Cologne when you go to the bank to ask for the loan.

CHARM, ALTAR PIECE, OR MOJO FOR GAMBLING

An Alligator Foot may be used as a lucky key-chain fob or pocket piece and fed with whiskey, urine, Hoyt's Cologne, or Van Van Oil to get it working. It is also a strong ingredient in any lucky hand, where it may be combined with two or more curios, such as a whole Nutmeg, Allspice Berries, Cinnamon Chips, Bayberry Chips, or a High John the Conqueror Root. It is the custom, if carrying it in a mojo bag or setting it on an altar, to jam in between the claws and secure with glue a paper bearing your money wishes written in red ink, either on plain paper or on a $2.00 bill.

THE SUCCESS SIGIL OR "MARKED MONEY"

The simplest spell i know for money drawing and general success in career was taught to me in the 1960s by the owner of a spiritual supply store in Oakland, California. All you need is a ball-point pen and Money Drawing Sachet Powder or Money Drawing Oil or Hoyt's Cologne. In a pinch you can use whiskey instead of the oil or cologne.

The "SUCCESS sigil" is a special, cryptic way of writing the word "success." Try it out on paper before you do it on your money. Write:

SUCCESS

Then write it again without the vowels, because we are only going to work with the consonants:

SCCSS

Add an S to the front of the word so that the whole thing is a symmetrical palindrome (reading the same from front to back and back to front):

SSCCSS

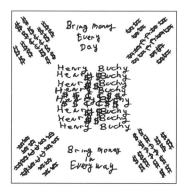

Then draw a line through each S to change it to a dollar sign $ and draw a line through each C to change it to a cent sign ¢:

$$¢¢$$

That is the SUCCESS sigil — **$$¢¢$$**.

Now that you know how to do it, take out every bill in your wallet. Write the **$$¢¢$$** sigil diagonally in every corner of each of the bills. Underneath the name of the US Treasurer, write your own full name.

Sprinkle the bills with Money Drawing Sachet Powder and drag your fingernails down them in "wavy snake lines," then shake the powder off. Dress the corners of each bill with a drop of Money Drawing Oil, Hoyt's Cologne, or whiskey as you say the 23rd Psalm (*"The Lord is my shepherd, i shall not want..."*). Put the dressed money back in your wallet.

You can also write the **$$¢¢$$** sigil in the form of a cross and use five of these crosses on a money-drawing petition, as Henry Buchy, a graduate of my Hoodoo Rootwork Correspondence Course, did above. His text is *"Bring Money Every Day / Bring Money in Every Way."*

A PAPER IN YOUR SHOE FOR A JOB INTERVIEW

This job is done for a client by a root doctor, and it was shown to me by a worker who knew her business, but i have taught others to do it for themselves. I will describe it as if you were helping a client and i trust you to make the necessary changes if you are doing the work for yourself.

Stand the client barefoot with her right foot upon a piece of paper if she is right-handed. If she is left-handed, stand her with her left foot on the paper. The best paper is tough, unprinted grocery sack paper, unless — and this is important — the job she wants is with a retail store that packages customers' goods in its own imprinted bags. As i was told, "If you want a job as a cashier at the Piggly Wiggly, get a paper bag from the Piggly Wiggly and stand right on their name, but if you want a job from the hardware store, go in and buy something and get one of their paper bags and stand right on that. Even if they use plain paper bags, stand on a bag that came from that store, if you want a position in that store."

Those instructions date from the 1970s, and since then i have added to this old method the idea that if the company is not a retail outlet, but does have an internet presence, you should print out a corporate web page with the company logo on it, especially a page that relates to the job you want.

Kneel down and trace around the client's foot with a pencil. Pray for the client as you do this. Cut out the shape of her foot, inside the line so that the paper is smaller than her actual foot and will fit in her shoe. On the paper, write out Luke 11:9, but insert the client's name and the name of the company in the scripture, so it looks like this:

> *And I say unto you,*
> Betty Ann Ransome Lewis,
> *Ask, and it shall be given you,*
> By the Piggly Wiggly in Jackson, Mississippi;
> *Seek, and ye shall find,*
> A job as a cashier or in the warehouse, either one;
> *Knock, and it shall be opened unto you,*
> In Jesus' name, Amen.

Draw dollar signs all around this prayerful petition and dress the paper with Steady Work Oil in the form of a cross. Tell the client to wear the paper in her shoe as she goes to the interview. Have her call you when the interview is scheduled so that you can keep a yellow light dressed with Steady Work Oil going for the date and time of the interview.

A PAPER UNDER A CANDLE FOR A JOB INTERVIEW

The same woman who showed me the previous spell gave the advice that the client was to be given a bottle of Steady Work Oil to bathe with and to rub the oil on her hands before meeting the interviewer at the job site. I followed her lead and told it this way for years. This was not a spell involving the use of papers, so i would not have included it here except as a footnote to the previous page, a mere add-on to the footprint spell.

However, when the book *"Hoodoo Bible Magic"* by Miss Michæle and Professor Charles Porterfield came out in 2014, i saw that they had coupled the same scripture i used (Luke 11:9) to another verse (Psalms 90:17), and this gave me the idea to couple their second verse to the second portion of the footprint spell, which involved the hand-treatment. So this is an example of how rootworkers influence one another over the years.

Miss Michæle and Professor Porterfield recommended Psalms 90:17 as a paper for the shoe, but the verse does not mention feet; rather it specifies the hands. The woman from Jackson, Mississippi, had taught me a hand-treatment, but she had given me no scripture for that portion of her work. Putting two and two together, i devised the following:

Trace the client's right hand if right-handed or left hand if left-handed onto a piece of paper. See the previous spell for how this should be done. Cut out the handprint and on it write Psalms 90:17: *"And let the beauty of the Lord our God be upon us: and establish thou the work of our hands upon us; yea, the work of our hands establish thou it."*

Have the client sign the Scriptural passage with her full name.

Open a small bottle of Steady Work Oil for her and pray this scripture over her hand as you dress the palm of her hand liberally with the oil, then place her hand down into her handprint to mark the hand outline as hers. Place the handprint paper face-up under a candle stand. Inscribe her name into the yellow candle (mentioned in the previous spell) which you will set as her job interview candle on the day and at the time she tells you to set it. Dress the candle with Steady Work Oil and give her the remainder of the bottle, with instructions to add a few drops to her bath and to anoint her hands with the oil as she says the portion of scripture every day up to and including the day of the interview.

I hope that you have enjoyed this glimpse into how an old, experienced worker such as myself creatively crafts spiritual patchwork from donated scraps. This one is a veritable friendship quilt across the decades.

PROTECT YOUR INVESTMENTS

If friends and relatives are always hitting on you for loans but are slow to repay, mix Sassafras, Cinnamon, Cloves, Irish Moss, and Alkanet in a green flannel bag. When a person asks to borrow from you, get two things from them — a hair from their head and their name on a little paper in their own handwriting. You don't need to explain why you want these things. Just say, "I'll loan you the money if i can have a hair from your head and your name written in your own handwriting on this little piece of paper." If they want the money bad enough, they'll do as you say. Write your name across their name on the paper to control them. Around the crossed names, in a square, write, *"Faithful to a Trust"* four times, once on each side of the square, like four square walls boxing the names in. Fold the paper towards you, around the hair, folding toward you again and again until it is small. Place the paper packet in the bag, and they will repay the loan on time.

QUICKSILVER GAMBLING CHARM UPDATED

People used to drill a hole in a Buckeye or a Nutmeg, fill it with liquid metallic Mercury or Quicksilver, and seal it with wax to carry as a lucky pocket piece. This is a health risk because Mercury is toxic. Instead, wrap a sigilized and written-on two dollar bill around the Buckeye or Nutmeg, and a Mercury Dime, folding it toward you to draw in money in games of chance.

MONEY AND A PHOTO FOR CHILD SUPPORT

If your child's father won't pay child support, cut a picture of him and the child apart and space it out with a dollar bill glued from behind the photo pieces. He will have to come across with that dollar before he can see the child. State as much by writing your monetary command in a straight line from his hands, across the money, and into the child's hands.

TO MAKE A LOVER MORE GENEROUS WITH MONEY

If you want your lover to be more forthcoming with money. add Chamomile to any love-drawing oils, powders, baths, perfumes, washes, or incenses and when you write your lover's name on paper use a dollar bill instead of brown paper or parchment to write on.

LOVE AND SEX SPELLS

Love drawing is, without a doubt, the most commonly-cited reason that people first learn how to use magic. There are tens of thousands of love spells in this world, of course, and not all of them involve papers — but when they do, the most common forms of papers will be name papers, photographs, papers as packets, papers as measures and true lengths, and paper dolls. Unless the layout and number of repetitions is stated, and the method of folding is specified, you may make your name paper as you feel most appropriate.

A SIMPLE MOJO TO ATTRACT LOVE

Write out a square name paper for the one whom you wish to attract. Fold it like a seed packet. In the packet place dried Rose petals, a pinch of Coriander seeds, and a Tonka Bean, plus a hair of the person, if you can get it. This packet is sufficient in itself to function as a hand, but if you want to preserve it for extended use, you may sew it into a square of red or pink cloth. Feed it with your own favourite perfume.

AN ARROW THROUGH THE HEART

This is simple love spell using just the Ace of Hearts from a regular deck of playing cards as your name paper: We've all seen a red Valentine's heart pierced by an arrow from upper left to lower right. It's a pretty universal symbol of love, so let's make a spell of it. Get an Ace of Hearts and a straight pin. With a Sharpie marker, write your lover's initials plus yours, like this:

NBY
+
CAY

Pierce the heart with the pin, as with an arrow, pray for love, and keep the card between your box springs and mattress. To be certain-sure that your lover will stay, use a safety pin instead of a straight pin. Thread something of your lover's and something similar of yours — a button, bead, scrap of handwriting, or piece of cloth — onto the safety pin for safekeeping, and the love between you will be truly held in place.

For many more playing card spells, please see this book:

"A Deck of Spells" by Professor Charles Porterfield

TO MAKE A MAN LOVE YOU AND STAY TRUE

This spell was published in 1974 by H. U. Lampe (Larry B. Wright) in his *Famous Voodoo Rituals and Spells*. Despite the title of the book, this is a hoodoo spell. Wright was not young when he wrote it, and both the techniques and wording show the influence of the 1936 book *Legends of Incense, Herb, and Oil Magic* by Lewis de Claremont, so i believe this is an early 20th century conjure spell. I have edited the text for clarity.

Obtain six red 9" jumbo candles, one candle holder that fits them, about 400 new pins, several sheets of parchment paper, a packet of Love Me Incense, an incense burner, a bottle of Dove's Blood brand red ink, a dip pen, and a bottle of Commanding Oil.

Cut out six equilateral triangle papers, three inches wide per side. These are to invoke the aid of the Trinity Power. Three is a powerful number and the three walled sides are believed to defend the ritual against negative forces while the three points attack evil in return. On each triangle write the name of the loved man three times with Dove's Blood Ink. Also prepare six squares of parchment paper with the name of the man written once on each, again using the Dove's Blood Ink.

Anoint one candle with Commanding Oil. The oil should be rubbed on from the center of the candle toward the top, then from the center of the candle toward the bottom. Take sixty pins and stick thirty into one side of the candle, starting at the bottom and making a straight line up to the top. Do the same on the other side. Stick the pins about halfway in. Heating them makes the work easier. Prepare each candle only at the time of using. Do not prepare the other candles ahead of time.

Place a paper triangle underneath the candle holder and light the candle at dusk. Once the candle is lit, also light the Love Me Incense. Put four pins through the first name parchment paper square, with the heads in the corners and the points toward the center, forming a figure X. Pass the pinned paper through the smoke of the incense. Place the smoked paper in front of the candle. Allow the candle to burn to the end.

The next morning gather the sixty pins, pass the parchment square through the smoke of newly lit Love Me Incense and then bury the paper and pins near your doorstep. This procedure is followed for six nights and mornings until the six candles have been burned. On the seventh night pour the remaining Commanding Oil upon the buried materials and make a strong wish that your lover will be true to you.

MICHELE JACKSON'S COWRIE SHELL FIDELITY SPELL

This spell to keep a man faithful uses a name paper as a physical measure — both a true length and a proxy. Michele writes:

"To keep your man faithful, you will need a large Cowrie Shell (at least 2½" long), a piece of paper 3" x 9", Calamus Root Chips, Knot Weed, Licorice Coot, Magnolia Leaf, Rosemary, his semen (or, if you can't get it, a 'male' oil like John the Conqueror or Nature Oil as a substitute), a piece of fabric cut from his underwear, a white offertory candle, four pink offertory candles, Stay With Me Oil, and a cloth to hold the shell on its back.

"Wash the shell and let it dry thoroughly. Take a measure of his penis. Get his semen unmixed with your fluids if you can. Cut a piece from your paper as long as his penis and 2" wide. It can be a plain rectangle, or you can make it anatomically correct. Write your petition for his fidelity on this paper down the middle, lengthwise. Rotate the paper 90 degrees and write your name over the petition nine times. Anoint the four corners and the center with his semen, or with the male oil.

"Anoint the opening of the shell with your sexual fluids.

"Grind the herbs and fabric small enough to fit into the shell. Place them in the shell while stating your petition. Put the paper in the shell as well. (If it is cut anatomically, put it in tip first.) Be sure to push it in deep enough so that none of it sticks out of the opening. This will help keep your man's private parts where they belong, safely inside your own genitalia.

"Light the white candle and drip wax into the shell's opening along its entire length to seal the materials inside. Work slowly; the shell will hold quite a bit of wax. Use this time to pray or speak your desires aloud. If wax flows out the ends, make a little nest of the wadded cloth and set the shell on its back on the cloth until the wax dries. You don't have to fill the shell to the brim — just full enough to keep the contents from moving about or leaking out of the opening. When the wax has dried, scrape any excess off with your fingernail and it will look like an ordinary Cowrie shell.

"Inscribe your wish on the pink candles and anoint them with Stay With Me oil, stating your petition or the 66th Psalm (*"Make a joyful noise unto God"*). Place the shell in the center of a square made with the four candles. Light the candles and let them burn down completely. Place the fixed shell near your bed, or between the box springs and mattress of your bed to keep his nature close to you at home. Breathe into the opening from time to time, or replenish the opening with your sexual fluids to keep it active."

A MAN'S MOJO HAND TO ATTRACT A LOVER FOR SEX

To prepare a strong love-drawing conjure hand, the man writes the woman's full name three times on a square of paper, rotates it a quarter-turn clockwise, and crosses it with his full name written three times. He gets one of the woman's hairs and one of his own hairs and folds them into square name paper, folding toward himself, to draw her to him, turning the paper a quarter-turn clockwise for positive results, and folding it again toward him. The paper is placed in a red flannel draw-string bag or sewn into a red flannel cloth packet, along with a single Sampson Snake Root and a pair of small Lodestone grits fed with Magnetic Sand.

This bag or packet can be dressed with Hoyt's Cologne, Attraction Oil, Follow Me Girl Oil, or Come To Me Oil, and the man should wear it in the front pocket, near the genitals. The Sampson Snake Root is a "male" root and the other ingredients are paired together to draw love.

Note that although this spell was taught to me as a man's spell to attract a woman and i have passed it along as i was given it, there is nothing in it that is inherently "female," because it places its emphasis entirely on the man's sexual prowess. For this reason it could just as easily be adapted to draw a male lover to a man, should such be his desire.

For male same-sex love, you may add Q Oil or Lavender Love Drops.

A WOMAN'S MOJO TO DRAW A MAN FOR LOVE

To make this little hand you will need the hair of the man you want. Pubic hair is best, but other hairs will do. Prepare a 3" square name-paper by using red ink to write the man's name over and over in the form of a spiral leading to the center of the paper, where you will draw a heart. Touch the heart with your sexual fluids. Use menstrual blood if you have it available; if it is gooey enough, stick the man's hair right in it.

Fold the paper by the corners-in method, and seal it with sticky red wax or glue. Dress the paper with Follow Me Boy Oil. Place it in a square of red flannel with a piece of Queen Elizabeth Root, two Red Rose Buds, two Lodestone Grits, Lavender Flowers, Spikenard, and other love curios, and sew the flannel into a packet small enough to wear on your person. Let your sweat get on it, then dress it with your own favourite perfume. If you wear it in your bosom, you will charm the man you desire with your special winning ways.

For female same-sex love, you may add Q Oil or Lavender Love Drops.

SPIKENARD AND BASIL FOR A HAPPIER MARRIAGE

Sprinkle dried Spikenard on an unframed photograph of the couple together that is cut in the shape of a heart, signed in the name of both parties, and buried face-up at the bottom of a flower pot or in a garden bed in which you grow a Basil plant. Spikenard promotes love and Basil promotes a happy marriage. Use the Basil in cooking food for both parties.

DOVES BLOOD INK AND SENNA TO ATTRACT LOVE

If you want to get to know someone who is unaware of your interest, write the person's name on a square of paper one time with Dove's Blood Ink and kiss it. Use the paper to fold a packet around some Senna leaves. You can use either the seed-packet method or the folded and tied method to create the packet. Place the packet in a red flannel bag, dress it with Come To Me Oil, and carry it on your person or in your purse.

AMERICAN MANDRAKE BOUND IN A NAME PAPER

Wire, tie, or glue American Mandrake roots to make a twig-doll, then wrap around its middle with a name paper bearing the beloved's name, and use it as a doll-baby for love. Brown paper bag paper is best, as it is strong and tough. Cut it to the person's measure, letter the name in black block letters with a red heart between each letter of the name.

ORANGE BLOSSOM WATER TO DRAW A MAN

Write the two names with pencil on separate papers and pin them together face-to-face. Put them into a pint jar of water with a spoonful of sugar or honey and a handful of Orange Blossoms. Loosely close the jar and surround it with five red candles dressed with Attraction Oil. Burn all the candles at once, calling the lover's name aloud as you light each one. Let the jar work for five days, then strain out the papers and flowers, bury them in a hole your back yard, under a Rose bush or at the foot of a tree, and dress the spot with the water and your own urine.

A BOSOM SACHET FOR LOVE

On a 3" paper square, write your lover's name corner to corner in red ink. Cross it corner-to-corner with your name. Add a pair of Blood Root Chips and a pinch each of Attraction and Love Me Powder. Fold it seed-packet style and sew it into red silk. Wear it in your bra as a bosom sachet.

MALE FERN TO ATTRACT A MAN

Women who want to draw a man's love have been known to write his name on paper, put it into a small envelope with Male Fern, and carry it in their purses.

A HONEY JAR SPELL TO RECONCILE AFTER A FIGHT

A hair of yours, a hair of your lover's, and a matched pair of Balm of Gilead Buds may be wrapped in a name paper bearing your estranged lover's name crossed by your name. The seed-packet style is good, because it will keep everything neat. Put the packet in a jar full of honey, syrup, or sugar. Burn a pink chime candle dressed with Reconciliation Oil on top of the jar every Monday, Wednesday, and Friday to sweeten your lover back to you. If you are physically apart, blend in equal parts of Return To Me Oil. Do not break any dripped wax off the jar; just let it build up and keep on burning the candles until you see some change.

TO CAUSE A COUPLE TO GET ALONG BETTER

Obtain a red Apple of a size that will fit inside an empty Coffee tin. On a square of paper no taller than the height of the Apple, write the squabbling couple's names, crossing them like an X. Around this X write the word "love" over and over again (lovelovelove) as many times as it takes to go around their names in an unbroken circle, never lifting your pen from the paper, and ending the final "e" so that it just runs into the first "l." It's okay to practice a few times to get this right — you want a perfectly done name paper. Core the Apple with a regular corer, making a hollow cylinder down the center. Roll the name paper into a tube, then slide it into the Apple, letting it expand to fill the space. Place the Apple in the Coffee tin, pour Cinnamon powder and a sweetener (sugar, syrup, honey, molasses, or whatever you prefer) into the hole, and put the lid on the tin. Hide the tin in a trunk or drawer, or bury it in the fighting couple's front yard. This will assist them to love one another again.

This spell has proved to be among the most popular that i first published in 2002 in my book on conjuring with herbs.

Read many more such herbal, mineralogical, and zoological spells in:

"Hoodoo Herb and Root Magic" by catherine yronwode

DEACON MILLETT'S SUGAR BOWL PACKETS

The following four spells by Deacon Millett are traditional domestic love spells. They are made in the kitchen, worked in a common sugar bowl, and hidden in plain sight. All four use a circular paper on which your name and your mate's are written three times and crossed, with the request written outside of the names, in a circle. Says Deacon Millett, "A sugar bowl on the table, used for coffee or tea, can be a center of sweetening for the home. The ideal bowl for our use is not flat-bottomed, but footed, with a hidden area beneath it which we can fill as we choose. Crafty folks affix green felt across the bottom, to hide the trick from view. But how many people are going to be looking under the sugar bowl?"

• A SUGAR BOWL FOR PEACE IN THE HOME

Place a pinch of Lavender, a pinch of Basil and a whole Clove in the center of your paper. Fold the paper toward yourself, to bring peace toward you. Turn it ninety degrees and fold it again. Continue until you have a tight "packet" with the names far inside.

• A SUGAR BOWL TO BRING TRUE LOVE

To turn a petition paper into a packet for romance, add a Rose Bud, a piece of Cinnamon Stick, and a piece of Cherry Bark. This packet takes more skill to fold, since it is chunkier. Tie it with red thread like you'd gift wrap a present to make it easier to hide beneath your sugar bowl.

• A SUGAR BOWL FOR A FAITHFUL MARRIAGE

Include a pinch of Coriander seed, a pinch of Cumin seed, and a single Red Clover flower in your packet. Women often add a sprig of Rosemary. Seeds tend to roll during packet folding, so take care!

• A SUGAR BOWL FOR RENEWED MARRIAGE VOWS

If your spouse has left home, tape your packet underneath the sugar bowl and place your wedding ring in the sugar bowl overnight to create sweet thoughts of your marriage. This was a favourite spell taught by Susie Bosselmann of the Lucky Mojo Curio Co., whose lady-hearted phone advice was a help to so many.

Read many more sweet spells for all types of situations in this book:
"Hoodoo Honey and Sugar Spells" by Deacon Millett

MISS MICHÆLE'S LOVE PRAYER BATH TRICKS

Miss Michæle, the proprietor of HoodooFoundry.com and the co-author of *Hoodoo Bible Magic*, contributes these dissolved-word spells:

- **AN INVISIBLE PRAYER IN A PICTURE FRAME**
  To influence someone for love, give them a gift of a picture in a frame. Take a love bath and use a little of the bath water as ink to write your love prayer on a plain piece of paper. Dry it and slip it behind the picture. The prayer will be invisible when dry — but only to the physical eye.

- **AN INVISIBLE PRAYER IN BATH WATER**
  Write your love prayer on paper in water-soluble ink, or even food colouring. Before bathing, take the paper with you into the tub, rinse the prayer right off into the water, bathe in it, and use the bath water to dress a gift you give to the one you love.

Read more spells by Miss Michæle in this book:
"Hoodoo Bible Magic" by Miss Michæle and Prof. C.D. Porterfield

DRAGON'S BLOOD INCENSE PACKET FOR MARRIAGE

Dragon's Blood powder is used by women who wish to receive an offer of marriage. The simplest way to do this is to write your lover's name one time on a small square of brown paper, cross it with your own name written one time. draw a heart in each quadrant of the paper, fold Dragon's Blood powder into the name paper, and throw the packet onto glowing charcoal along with Love Me Incense while saying a prayer. Do this every night while the Moon is waxing or as long as you see progress being made. You may add Deer's Tongue leaf to the packet if the man seems shy to speak.

TO STOP MARITAL FIGHTING

Wrap a small amount of Vandal Root (caution: it is very stinky!) and a photo that shows both you and your spouse together in a piece of brown paper. Carry this odiferous packet for three days and then take out the all of the Vandal Root and throw it into running water, to take the fighting away. Replace it with Lovage Root and keep that with the picture thereafter.

FOR THE RETURN OF AN ABSENT LOVER

This is not a spell to bring back a lover after a fight or break up; rather it is to return someone who has moved away or is travelling.

Write your absent lover's name on paper nine times and cross it with your name written nine times. Place the name paper in a white saucer and fill the saucer with white sugar, covering the paper. Buy nine small white candles and burn one, set upright in the sugar, each day for nine days.

If your lover has not returned after nine days, burn everything in a fire and start again with new materials, repeating the process nine more days. If your lover still does not come back, again burn everything, and make a third attempt. If this spell does not work after three tries, your lover will not return.

TO CAUSE A COUPLE'S LOVE TO GROW

This spell is not generally performed by the people involved but is done on their behalf by a third party, either a family member or a professional root worker.

Get a Red Delicious Apple and a clay flower pot large enough that the Apple will fit inside with lots of room to spare. You will also need a small living Fern plant. The species of Fern does not matter, but Maidenhair Fern and Male Fern are the two species most often used in love spells.

On a square of paper no taller than the height of the Apple, write out the couple's full names, crossing them like an X. Around this X write your wish for their love and happiness, over and over again (e.g. loveoneanotherloveoneanother) as many times as it takes to go around their names in an unbroken circle, never lifting your pen from the paper and ending the final letter of the last word so that it just runs into the first letter of the first word. Practicing this with a pencil on a scrap of paper a few times is fine, in order to get a neat final version.

Core the Apple to make a hollow cylinder down the center. Roll the name paper into a tube, then slide it into the Apple, letting it expand to fill the void. Place the Apple in the flower pot, pour Cinnamon powder and sweetener into the hole (sugar, syrup, honey, or molasses, as you prefer), and top it off with regular potting soil. Plant the Fern with its roots in the soil on top of the Apple and water it with Holy Water. As the Fern grows, so will the couple's love for one another grow. It should only be watered with Holy Water as long as you wish to work the spell.

A LOVING FATHER FOR YOUR CHILD

Many a single mother has found herself cursing the no-good man who won't support his child. Sweetening the situation will help a man want to take care of his family, and you should try it before trying to take the man to court and causing a rift in the life of the child. I have a special petition paper for such cases.

Use the mama and the daddy names written nine times each, side by side in two columns (because they are no longer a couple) and the baby name crossed over both, holding them all together. Then, around and around the names write, *"We are family, forever and in all ways, and let no one put this family asunder."* In the corners of the paper, draw four eye-shapes, just the outlines, with no pupils in the centers. Inside each eye-shape draw a heart, and inside each heart draw a dollar sign. The meaning of this symbol in each corner is *God is watching you* (the eye shape) — *so love the child* (the heart) *and pay the money* (the dollar sign).

HONEY JAR FOR SWEETENING SOMEONE

A small glass honey jar in which a person's name paper is placed (wrapped around a paper with a wish and the person's hair, if it can be had) is used as a base upon which to burn candles for a variety of sweet purposes, from attracting a new lover or reconciling with an old one to influencing a judge to favour one's court case or a boss to grant one's request for a raise. You can add herbs to the packet too: Rose Petals for love, Little John to Chew for court matters, or Fenugreek Seeds for money.

You can also use white or brown sugar, jelly, or jam in the jar. Some workers fill the jar with molasses, corn syrup, or cane syrup, depending on what they have at hand, the type of case they are trying to work, or the skin-colour of the person they are trying to influence.

The candles burned atop the jar lid are colour-keyed to your intentions: white for blessings, stopping gossip, or finding a new love; pink for romance and reconciliation; red for sex, love, and pleasure; brown for court cases; blue for peace in the home; green when asking for a raise or seeing a bank officer about a loan, and yellow for success.

Read many more types of sweetening spells in this book:
"Hoodoo Honey and Sugar Spells" by Deacon Millett
Read much more about the history of sweeting spells online:
LuckyMojo.com/honeyjar.html

"LOVE ME OR DIE": TO GOOFER A MAN FOR LOVE

This is a jack ball for coercive love that was related to me by a 50-55 year old woman customer in a candle store on Maxwell Street in Chicago in 1965. She said, "If you want a man to love you, and he absolutely refuses, you can goofer him to love you — you know, make him sick to love you." This is her recipe:

You will need his hair, your hair, a small High John the Conqueror Root, Goofer Dust (or Graveyard Dirt), Love Me Sachet Powder, a piece of brown paper (torn on all four sides from a paper bag), a waterproof pen that writes red, a waterproof pen that writes black, a brand-new spool of red sewing thread, a red flannel bag, and a sharp pen knife.

On the paper, write his full name seven times in black ink, then rotate the paper and print "*LOVE ME OR DIE*" over his name seven times in red ink, crossing it and covering it. Set the name paper aside. Use the pen knife to carve a slit-shaped hole in the High John Root and wedge your hair and his hair in there together. Then pack the slit tight with a mixture of Goofer Dust and Love Me Sachet Powder. Thoroughly wet the name paper with your urine and wrap it around the High John Root, pressing and forming it as you would papier-mâché, to keep the hairs and powders inside. While it is still wet, wrap it up in the brand-new red thread, going round and around very neatly, like a ball of twine, until the paper is entirely covered. When you are done, tie the thread off with seven knots, and leave a length of thread to hang it from. You can double or triple the hanging-thread for strength, and finish it with a loop for your finger.

Carry the prepared charm in a red flannel bag and moisten it with your urine when needed. Hold it by its hanging-thread to "operate" it, swinging it back and forth, or round and around toward you, as you call the man's name to draw him to you. Get a rhythm going and say his name, like this, over and over: *"[First Name, Last Name], love me or die; [First Name, Last Name], love me or die; [First Name, Last Name], love me or die."*

"You do this," the woman told me, "and the man will either love you, or he'll get real sick. If he gets sick, don't let up; just keep your urine wet on that thing; just keep working with it. That's the way you get him, you weaken him. When he is about finished, you can nurse him back to health. Then he's all yours."

COURT CASE SPELLS

TO GET A COURT CASE DISMISSED

If you are being brought to court on false charges, this is an old way to get your case dismissed. Do not try it if you are actually guilty; this spell is for the innocent only.

Using a waterproof marker, write the names of all Twelve Apostles on a Sage, Bay, or Plantain Leaf. Their names are Simon Peter, Andrew, James son of Zebedee, John, Philip, Bartholomew, Thomas, Matthew; James son of Alphæus, Judas Thaddæus; Simon the Canaanite, and Judas Iscariot. Place this in your right shoe.

Write the name of the judge on paper, and place this in your left shoe. It is said that if you wear these in your shoes, your appearance will be delayed, and the third time you go, your case will be dismissed.

A FIVE-HERB COURT CASE MOJO

If you oppose others in court, whether as plaintiff or defendant, write all of your opponents' names on paper, cross them with your name written nine times, wrap the name paper around a Little John to Chew Root and dress the packet with Court Case Oil. Place the packet in a cloth or letter bag with Calendula, Cascara Sagrada, Dill Seed, Deer's Tongue Leaf, and Oregano.

A SEVEN-HERB COURT CASE MOJO IN A PAPER

Write the Names of those who oppose you on a piece of brown grocery bag paper and cross their names with your Name written three times. Wrap a pinch each of Calendula, Anise Seed, Deer's Tongue, Celery Seed, Tobacco snuff, Cascara Sagrada, and Dill Seed in the name paper, folding away from you and saying, *"May this trouble be removed from me."* Tie the packet with thread and carry it in your pocket when you go to court. In the courtroom, chew a Little John Root and spit it onto the paper-wrapped mojo hand to feed it.

TO SWEETEN A JUDGE

This spell came from one of Harry Hyatt's interviewees in the 1930s:

To get a judge on your side, write his or her name nine times and place the paper with Cinnamon and sugar in your left shoe. Now you have the judge under your feet and working for you.

FROZEN SEEDS TO FREEZE COURT CASES

Write the names of all the parties on paper in red ink, wrap the paper in red cloth, and sprinkle it with Dill seeds and Coriander seeds. Keep this charm in a cold, dark place — or freeze it in a block of water — for nine days before the court date, or until you have won.

SEVEN OF CLUBS TO CONFUSE COURT PROCEEDINGS

This spell comes from Professor Charles Porterfield: "To sow confusion among the witnesses and prosecuting attorneys, take the Seven of Clubs and write your name across the middle Club with the words 'Go free' beneath it. Then write the names of the prosecuting attorneys and witnesses on the card and strike them through. Finally, draw an X over the remaining six Clubs, dress the card with Inflammatory Confusion Oil, and place it into an envelope with Poppy seeds and Black Mustard seeds. Seal the envelope and write the date and time of the court hearing on it. Carry this on you in a pocket when you go into court. It will cause disruptive confusion among the prosecution lawyers and witnesses."

TIE PEOPLE TOGETHER TO CATCH THEM CHEATING

If a man believes his wife is cheating, he can go to the woods, select two lengths of wild Grape vine from one plant, and name one for his wife and the other for the man whom he suspects. He writes his wife's name on top of the man's on a brown paper with a pencil, urinates on the paper to soften it, sprinkles it with Red Pepper, wraps it tightly around the two vines like a bandage, and ties it up tight with one of his own shoelaces. He then goes directly home, where, if she is cheating, he will find his wife and her lover stuck together like two Dogs. He can take a photo and bring a divorce suit.

BEEF TONGUE SPELL TO SHUT THEM UP

Cross the names of all opposing lawyers or witnesses with your name written nine times or with the command SHUT YOUR MOUTH! nine times to cross and cover them. Sprinkle the paper with red hot Cayenne Pepper powder and say, "May your words burn in your mouth if you speak against me." Slit a beef tongue open, stuff the paper in, and pin or sew the tongue shut. Freeze it in your freezer until the court date.

You can read more about beef tongue court case spells online here:
LuckyMojo.com/courtcase.html

UNCROSSING SPELLS

TO REMOVE PROBLEMS AND BAD HABITS

Obtain something small to symbolize the problem or bad habit you wish to be rid of. On a small square of paper, write a description of the problem in your own words, very simply, such as "addiction to nicotine," "irrational craving for Burger King Whoppers," or "kleptomania." Do not use words like "my" or "i" in the description; you do not want to own this problem; you want to get rid of it!

If your problem is alcoholism, write out the description of the problem with a pencil and dip the paper in the alcohol, then let it dry. If you can soak a paper label off a bottle of the alcohol, use that to write upon.

If your problem is drug or cigarette addiction, wrap a bit of the drug or Tobacco product that is hurting you in the paper on which you have written the description. Use a product label to write on, if one is available.

If the problem is purely mental, and concerns your thoughts, obtain a graphic representation of the mental problem, such as a screaming face to symbolize uncontrolled anger. Crumple it up into a little ball and wrap it in the description paper.

Mix Knot Weed with soft beeswax of the kind that comes in sheets for beekeepers to use. (The exact item you want is called "100% beeswax thin surplus foundation for square section comb honey.") If you cannot find Knot Weed, the same spell can be done using Couch Grass or any species of runner-grass to wind around the ball to bind it. If you cannot find beeswax, use yellow cheese rind wax such as that on Laughing Cow Bonbel Babybel Edam cheese. Speak aloud your desire for your problems to be gone the entire time that you form the wax and herbs into a ball around the written paper with the object inside.

Bury the ball in a graveyard and ask the spirits of the dead to keep your problem until you return. If you come from a family where the type of problem you need to overcome is prevalent, that is, if your ancestors may have had the same problem, do not go to the grave of an ancestor for help in this matter. Instead, go to the grave of a minister, an upright businessman, or, best of all, someone who had this problem and overcame the problem in life. Pay three coins to the spirit for this service. Lay them out in a triangle and bury the ball in the middle of the triangle, then bury the three coins where they lay. Walk away and don't look back.

PROTECTION SPELLS

EMERGENCY PROTECTION IN A SHOE OR A POCKET

If you must go into a place where there is reason to fear a physical attack, you can protect yourself by carrying Psalms 91. Most folks write out the Psalm by hand — but if you don't have time, just photocopy this page! This Psalm promises that God will protect you, *"lest thou dash thy foot against a stone,"* so some folks wear it in their shoe. It also promises that the Lord's truth *"shall be thy shield and buckler,"* so other folks wear it in a breast pocket. Either way is fine. Or you can carry two copies of it.

==

Psalms 91: 1 He that dwelleth in the secret place of the most High shall abide under the shadow of the Almighty. 2 I will say of the LORD, He is my refuge and my fortress: my God; in him will I trust. 3 Surely he shall deliver thee from the snare of the fowler, and from the noisome pestilence. 4 He shall cover thee with his feathers, and under his wings shalt thou trust: his truth shall be thy shield and buckler. 5 Thou shalt not be afraid for the terror by night; nor for the arrow that flieth by day; 6 Nor for the pestilence that walketh in darkness; nor for the destruction that wasteth at noonday. 7 A thousand shall fall at thy side, and ten thousand at thy right hand; but it shall not come nigh thee. 8 Only with thine eyes shalt thou behold and see the reward of the wicked. 9 Because thou hast made the LORD, which is my refuge, even the most High, thy habitation; 10 There shall no evil befall thee, neither shall any plague come nigh thy dwelling. 11 For he shall give his angels charge over thee, to keep thee in all thy ways. 12 They shall bear thee up in their hands, lest thou dash thy foot against a stone. 13 Thou shalt tread upon the lion and adder: the young lion and the dragon shalt thou trample under feet. 14 Because he hath set his love upon me, therefore will I deliver him: I will set him on high, because he hath known my name. 15 He shall call upon me, and I will answer him: I will be with him in trouble; I will deliver him, and honour him. 16 With long life will I satisfy him, and shew him my salvation.

==

PROTECTIVE WATER OR COLOGNE OF PSALMS 91

Just as Psalms 91 can be carried on the person, so can its essence be transmitted into liquids for use in protection of a person or a location. Write Psalms 91 on white paper in water-soluble ink. (You cannot use a photocopy for this.) Here are two things you can do next:

Dip the paper in a glass of water to dissolve the ink in the water. Wad up the paper and swallow it like a pill, with a swig of the water to get it down. Use the rest of the water in a bath. This will protect you inside and out.

Place the paper in a bottle of cologne, Chinese Wash, or water. Let it stay in there and dissolve. Use the liquid as you normally would on your body, as a misted room fragrance, as scrub water for house cleaning, or however you like. The liquid will convey the protection of the 91st Psalm everywhere you spread, spray, or splash it.

POLICEMAN'S NAME FOR PROTECTION OF PROPERTY

Go to the graveyard of a policeman. He should have been a fair and honest man, preferably one known to you in life. If he lived and died heroically, so much the better. You can research him on the internet, though online obituary sites, or find-a-grave services. When you get to the right policeman's grave, stand there and speak with him. Tell him you have one more job for him to do, and ask his consent. If he gives it, purchase a handful of his graveyard dirt by paying for it with nine copper pennies. (A slang term for policemen is "coppers" or "cops.")

Write out Psalms 91 by hand and sign the policeman's name at the bottom of the paper, as if he were the author of the Psalm. Burn a packet of Fiery Wall of Protection Incense to ash. (To speed this process, you may burn it on a charcoal tablet.) As it burns, set the prayer and name paper alight in the incense, and make sure it is consumed utterly to ashes.

Mix the incense and prayer paper ashes with the graveyard dirt of the policeman and walk around the perimeter of your property, calling his name and asking him to protect you and your home as you sprinkle the dirt on the ground. Many old-timers, myself included, would tell you to walk backwards as you do this, casting the dirt to your front, with a very slight side to side motion, as if you were broadcasting seeds in a field.

When you have circled the entire property and sprinkled out all of the ash and dirt mixture, stop and recite the entirety of Psalms 91 one more time, and close with *"Amen."*

PROTECTION FOR A HOME OR AN ILLEGAL BUSINESS

Wash your business or home doorstep down with your own first urine of the day, diluted into a bucket of water, then sprinkle red brick dust on the doorstep to keep out unwanted people.

To make this scrub much stronger, write the name of the Captain of Police on paper, burn the name paper to ashes, and add the crumbled ashes to your scrub water. In this way, the officers who patrol your beat under that Captain of Police will know that your place is protected "in his name" and they will not bother you.

PROTECTING MONEY FROM THEFT

If you are the kind of person who keeps cash money in the home and you are afraid it will be stolen, this method of protecting it will be of service. It combines several ways of working in one trick.

Mark each piece of paper currency with your initials. You may write your initials anywhere on the bills, but always be consistent about where you place the mark, and do not use the corners, because these can be clipped off by a thief and the bill will still be valid currency. The best place to initial the currency is under the name of the Secretary of the Treasury, whose office and function will then protect your money

Place a folded paper packet of Gall of the Earth Root amongst the currency. If you cannot get Gall of the Earth, Sassafras and Alkanet are suitable substitutes for it in this spell. Place it in the middle of the pack.

For additional protection, write out the first verse of Psalms 91 (*"He that dwelleth in the secret place of the most High shall abide under the shadow of the Almighty"*) on just one of the pieces of paper currency and shuffle it somewhere into the stack, thus placing it "in the most secret place" even from yourself.

Hide the entire pack of currency well, and no one will touch it.

PSALMS 121 AGAINST NIGHTMARES AND HAG-RIDING

If you are troubled by nightmares or hag-riding, write out Psalms 121 on paper or get a printed copy. Place it under a glass of water, which you will keep on your bedside nightstand. Before you go to sleep, invite all spirits of the night to come and drink, before they enter your dreams. Once they do, they will be trapped in the water and will leave you alone. When you awaken, throw the water out and wipe the glass clean.

SUSAN BARNES' EPHESIANS 6:11-20 FOR PROTECTION

This protection charm utilizes the verses of Ephesians 6:11-20. *("Put on the whole armour of God, that ye may be able to stand against the wiles of the devil")*. Susan explains how to make and use it:

"Write or photocopy the text from your Bible or find it online and print it out." (The copy included on this page should be photocopied at 50%.)

"Surround the text with the phrase *"protectmeprotectmeprotectme"* hand-written all around it as a square border. Pray over the petition, then apply a five-spot of Fiery Wall of Protection Oil to it. In the center of the petition, place a small personal concern, such as a nail clipping or hair, of yourself or the person for who you are making the charm.

"Smoke the petition with Fiery Wall of Protection Incense. Fold and turn and fold the petition toward you at least four times to make a small packet. Smoke the shoe of your dominant foot (or your client's shoe) with Fiery Wall of Protection Incense, and place the petition in the shoe. Once folded, it is fairly small and should fit into the toe of the shoe."

==

Ephesians 6:11 Put on the whole armour of God, that ye may be able to stand against the wiles of the devil. 12 For we wrestle not against flesh and blood, but against principalities, against powers, against the rulers of the darkness of this world, against spiritual wickedness in high places. 13 Wherefore take unto you the whole armour of God, that ye may be able to withstand in the evil day, and having done all, to stand. 14 Stand therefore, having your loins girt about with truth, and having on the breastplate of righteousness; 15 And your feet shod with the preparation of the gospel of peace; 16 Above all, taking the shield of faith, wherewith ye shall be able to quench all the fiery darts of the wicked. 17 And take the helmet of salvation, and the sword of the Spirit, which is the word of God: 18 Praying always with all prayer and supplication in the Spirit, and watching thereunto with all perseverance and supplication for all saints; 19 And for me, that utterance may be given unto me, that I may open my mouth boldly, to make known the mystery of the gospel, 20 For which I am an ambassador in bonds: that therein I may speak boldly, as I ought to speak. Amen.

==

CROSSING SPELLS

A PAPER DOLL IN A COFFIN

This curse is adapted from one taught by Larry B. Wright, a.k.a. H.U. Lampe. I have used it successfully, but in doing so, i modified it greatly: Prepare a small matchbox coffin. Paint or mark it black all over, inside and out. Cut out a paper doll and name it for the person. It must be no wider than the matchbox is long. Try to capture the look of the person in silhouette form. Use black paper if you wish. If you have a full-length photo of the person, use that instead, trimming it around the edges of the person's body — but it must be on plain paper, not photo paper.

Write the person's name vertically with Bat's Blood Ink in block letters from the head of the paper doll to the feet, one letter under the next. Stick a brand new sewing pin into the paper doll's head and thread it in and out of the paper to the feet, accordion-folding the paper as you go. Try to stab the pin through every letter of the person's name. The paper will fold up very tight and small if you do this carefully. Place the image and pin in the match box. You may stab the end of the pin out through the matchbox to hold everything in place. Carry the box to a graveyard and dig a hole for it, but not in the grave of anyone already buried there, for this is its own grave. On top of the box place an X of Devil's Shoe String Roots to tangle and hold the person down. Sprinkle the roots and box with Black Arts Oil, then cover it over with dirt. Leave the graveyard by a route different than the way you came, and never return to the spot where you buried the box.

TO PUT THE JINX ON SOMEONE

Here's another spell by Larry B. Wright: Write your enemy's name diagonally from corner to corner on a square piece of paper, forming an X. Pointing inward from the four center-edges of the paper draw four arrow-shapes. They should point to the place where the names cross. At the center make a small pile of dried powdered Dog shit, Black Pepper, and Gunpowder taken from a bullet or a firecracker. Fold the paper inward from the corners and secure it with thread or string. Hide it in the enemy's yard, house, or place of business to cause bad luck. The smaller you make the packet, the easier it will be to hide.

RUN DEVIL RUN PACKET TO CHASE AN ENEMY AWAY

This is a highly modified version of an old spell taught by Larry B. Wright in the 1970s. If you cannot use a traditional Hot Foot Powder spell on your enemy's foot-track, try this instead; it may work for you. Write the name of your enemy thirteen times on a square piece of paper and on it place a pinch each of Run Devil Run Powder, Hot Foot Powder, Sulphur Powder, and Epsom Salts. Fold it by bringing the corners to the center, and then doing so a second time. Seal it by dripping wax from a red candle dressed with Damnation Oil onto the center and the folds. Bury the sealed packet in the ground for thirteen days as the Moon wanes. Every night wet the burial spot with Damnation Oil. On the fourteenth night, at the dark of the Moon, dig up the packet, burn it to ashes and scatter the ashes to the winds at a crossroads.

WETTED, DRIED, WAXED, AND GOOFERED

Here is more old-fashioned work by Larry B. Wright, who had a knack for curses. Again i present the spell as i myself modified it for use:

Write your enemy's name every which way with no rhyme or reason and in no straight lines, all over both sides of a piece of paper. Wet the paper in a dish of Four Thieves Vinegar. Take out the paper and put it in a safe place to dry. Fold and roll the dried paper into a small cylinder and completely cover it with red wax dripped from a candle dressed with Crossing Oil. Hide or bury the waxed roll in the enemy's yard. After three days sprinkle War Water on his or her front steps as you walk by at night. Two nights after that, throw Crossing Powder from the steps to the yard. The following night sprinkle Goofer Dust all along the sidewalk.

TO SUBDUE AN OPPONENT OR COMPETITOR

I got the idea for this curse from Larry B. Wright, but i have changed it so greatly that it is as much my own as his by this time:

Rub Essence of Bend-Over Oil on the shoes of the one you wish to subdue, but if you cannot touch the shoes directly, write his or her name seven times on a piece of paper and drench it in the oil to use as a proxy. Burn the paper to ash and spread the ashes in the victim's pathway as you recite Psalms 43:3 (*"He will subdue the peoples under us, and the nations under our feet"*) three times. Repeat this entire process on a total of five separate occasions, for a total of fifteen repetitions of the Psalm.

A RED PEPPER PACKET TO UNDERMINE AN ENEMY

To slowly and subtly weaken an enemy or competitor, fold Red Pepper, whole Black Pepper Corns, and Graveyard Dirt into a piece of paper on which you have written the enemy's name and birthdate. Fold this name paper packet into a piece of black cloth, such as a mourner's pocket handkerchief, tie it with black thread, and hide it in the enemy's house, car, or place of business. The enemy will slowly weaken.

TO SEND AN ENEMY AWAY

Write your enemy's name with a pencil on a Black Hen's egg and soak the egg for nine days in Four Thieves Vinegar to which you have added Red Pepper and Black Salt. At midnight of the ninth day, carry the egg to a crossroads and, holding the egg in your hand, dance around the forks of the road, cursing your enemy, and sending your hatred into the egg. At the climax of your dance, throw the egg sharply to the ground, breaking it, then walk away silently and quietly, and don't look back.

STRONG JINX ON AN ENEMY

Mix dried Snake Head herb with Crossing Incense, call your enemy's name, and light it. As it burns, write your enemy's full name backwards nine times in black ink on a sheet of paper that is torn on all four sides, sprinkle it with Goofer Dust, wrap it around Snake Head herb and Snake shed powder, place the bundle in a raggedly-torn black cloth, and tie it with black thread. Bury the packet in a graveyard and your enemy will get sick.

GUNPOWDER TO DRIVE AN ENEMY AWAY

Pick up your enemy's left foot-track, mix it with Sulphur Powder and Gunpowder, and put the mixture on a piece of brown paper. Light all four corners of the paper with a match and step back. It will blow up and your enemy will be forced to leave town. Another way to do this is to shoot the enemy's name with a bullet.

TO KEEP SOMEONE IN JAIL

Write the person's name on paper and put it into a bowl with Red Pepper, Black Pepper, a nail, and a door key. Pour in 1/4 cup ammonia and set a second door key upright in the bowl, resting against the side. Every day at noon, turn the upright key to keep the person locked up.

FOUR WAYS TO BREAK A COUPLE UP

This is a family of related spells based around the employment of name papers, vinegar, and sharp, pointed things. After that, they differ: Write each party's name nine times on a piece of paper. Wad each paper into a ball around a hair from that party. Put the two wads into a narrow bottle with nine nails, nine pins, and nine needles facing every which way to keep the papers from touching. Fill the bottle with vinegar and shake daily.

A second way is to write the names on two separate papers, fold them around hairs or personal concerns and put them in a bottle with Black Dog Hair, Black Cat Hair, nine Pins, nine Needles, nine Coffin Nails, Hot Foot Powder, Goofer Dust, Graveyard Dirt, Sulphur, and Red Pepper. Fill the bottle with Four Thieves Vinegar or your urine and bury it at their doorstep.

A third way is to write the names on one paper, not touching, and cut the names apart, after which they must not be allowed to touch. In each paper, place a hair of each party. Add Black Dog Hair and Black Cat Hair, either one type of animal hair in each ball of paper, or one type at each end of the jar. The Cat and Dog hair make them fight like Cats and Dogs. Shake the bottle daily, and after nine days, add your urine to "piss on them" and your poo to "shit on them" and throw the bottle at their house, hard enough to break it.

A fourth way starts with a single paper bearing both of their names, not touching. Cut the paper in half, separating the names, then write commands like *"Fight! Quarrel! Separate! Divorce!"* across the names, every which way. Fill the bottle with nails, needles, pins, broken razor blades, and broken glass, keeping the names apart. Top it up with Four Thieves Vinegar and black ink. Poke a tiny hole in the lid with a nail before you screw it on and bury the bottle upside down in their pathway so that they have to walk over it as the liquid drips out very slowly, killing their relationship.

There are more ways this spell could be worked by choosing different elements from among the methods described. Feel free to improvise.

BOILING NAME-PAPERS TO CATCH A THIEF

If something has been stolen and you want to find the thief, write the name of each suspect in pencil on a piece of brown paper. Fill a pot with salty water and put the first name-paper in. Boil it until the water evaporates, leaving a salty crust. If that person is the thief, he will contact you while the water boils. If you are not contacted, add new water to the pot, remove the first name and boil the next. The one who contacts you while his name is boiling is the thief.

HOW TO BURN A BLACK VIGIL LIGHT FOR A BREAK UP

If you are setting black glass-encased Break Up or Separation Vigil Candles, you can take a clue from the Break Up bottles described previously. Do not burn the candle on a single name paper, face-down, as you would to jinx or cross an enemy. Instead, prepare their names as you would for the bottle spell, either by starting with two separate pieces of paper or by writing their names on a single paper, not touching, and cutting it apart. I prefer to use the single paper for this, cutting it apart with pinking shears, which make a zig-zag cut, to separate the names. You could also tear the names apart, or use regular scissors in a zig-zag, jagged motion. You may add commands, as described in the fourth of the bottle spell variations, by using words like *"Fight! Quarrel! Separate! Divorce!"* across the names, written helter skelter and every which way.

Once you have the two name papers, you need to decide if, after the break up of their relationship, you want both parties to go away and out of your life, or if you want one to stay and one to leave. Whoever you want to have leave, fold that person's name paper away from you, cursing the person by name. Two folds is sufficient. Whoever you want to have stay, fold that person's name toward you, commanding the person to remain with you. Again, two folds is sufficient.

Tape the papers to each side of the glass. Position the one you want to leave so that the fold is at the top and the edges point downward. Position the one you want to stay so that the fold is at the top and the edges point upward. Dress the candle with Break Up or Separation Oil, as you wish.

BREAK UP SPELL WITH A LEMON

Light a black altar light or offertory candle dressed with Confusion Oil and cut a fresh lemon in half. Write the names of the two parties as shown (back-to-back) and cut the names apart with pinking shears.

Place the name papers back-to-back inside the Lemon, with Black Dog Hair, Black Cat Hair, and Red Pepper between them. Tie the Lemon up with black thread, seal it by dripping black candle wax all over it, and bury it in the couple's yard, so they will be sour-tempered and fight like Cats and Dogs.

Variants of this spell specify submerging the Lemon in a jar of Four Thieves Vinegar to sour the relationship even more or putting it in a jar of Black Cow's milk to curdle and clabber their lives.

OLD-FASHIONED BLACK CANDLE REVENGE SPELL

Cut the top off a black jumbo candle, turn it upside down, and carve a new tip at what was the bottom. Carefully heat it a section at a time and press 99 whole Pepper Corns into it, all over the surface. Place it in a saucer on top of the enemy's face-down name paper and dress it by pouring a whole bottle of Crossing Oil over it. At midnight, carry this mess to a deserted crossroads or, if possible, to the enemy's yard while he or she is away. Set it down in the middle of a large X inside a circle made by walking backward while sprinkling Crossing Powder diagonally from one corner of the crossroads or yard to the other, and then around the X in a circle. As the candle burns, speak a detailed list of the enemy's sins aloud, followed by the your requirements for true, justified, and lasting retribution.

JINX AN ENEMY AND HIS CAR WITH A BLACK CANDLE

Write your enemy's name on his photo and completely cover his name with repeated commands for car trouble. Set the photo face-down under a black jumbo candle on which you have carved your enemy's name with a Coffin Nail. Dress the candle with Black Arts Oil. Burn the candle for 15 minutes every night and burn Vandal Root with Black Arts Incense on charcoal next to the candle every night. Hide Vandal Root in his car, so that he will wreck or have bad luck with the car.

TO STOP AN ENEMY'S LUCK AND SEND HIM AWAY

Place a handful of Knot Weed, one Devil's Shoe String Root, and the enemy's picture or name paper on a black mourner's handkerchief. Dress it with Crossing Powder, and tie it into a bundle with black thread. Every day for three days, step on it and say, *"[Name], may your luck go away"* three times. On the fourth day, throw it into a river and say, *"As this bundle goes away, so will [Name] go away."*

TO DRIVE SOMEONE INSANE

Get a hair from your enemy's head and write out a name paper on which his or her name is copied out nine times. Put these things into a bottle with the juice of a Lemon. Shake up the bottle as you say a curse, then set it upside-down along the East side (the sunrise side) of the enemy's house. As the Sun goes from East to West, the person's mind will be soured and carried down toward sunset, and depression or insanity will result.

STINGING INSECTS AND SHARP POINTS AGAINST A FOE

Write your enemy's name on paper, add any personal concerns or other identifiers, and seal it up in a bottle with Dauber Dirt powder from nine different Dirt Dauber Wasp nests, plus nine needles, nine pins, nine tacks, and nine Red Ants.

Every day at noon, shake the bottle up and call your enemy's name nine times, making nine curses for his ruin. Do this for nine days, with full faith and confidence that your wish for his destruction will come to pass.

A FREEZER SPELL TO MESS UP A MAN'S SEXUALITY

Use a large dill pickle to represent the man's penis. (In case you are wondering, a pickle is better than a mild Cucumber or Zucchini for this trick, because it is sour and will sour his sex life.) Slit the Pickle, then insert his semen or his urine on a name paper that you have cut to the measure of his penis, and sprinkle Alum powder on it to stop him from coming or from peeing. Add Red Pepper to give him a burning inflammation of the penis and Black Mustard seeds to harm his sexuality and his urinary tract.

These are traditional minerals, roots, and barks from our long past history and give real power to the work. Why Alum powder? Try it on your tongue and be convinced as to why it shuts things up.

Also be fully aware that if you do this, the man won't be having sex with you either, and he may get seriously ill from urinary blockage. You will have frozen his penis. This is a grievous spell, and the intention is harmful, so the work must be carefully performed and you'd better be prepared to tell God why you did it.

A FREEZER SPELL TO MESS UP A WOMAN'S SEXUALITY

To freeze a woman's sex drive, give her an infection, and stop her ability to bear children, slit open a Fig or Pear, and insert into it her menstrual blood or her urine on a name paper made to be the measure of her privates. Sprinkle in Alum powder to stop her periods, Red Pepper to give her a burning inflammation of the genitals, and Black Mustard seeds to harm her sexuality and her urinary tract.

This sexually damaging freezer spell can be wrapped up in aluminum foil, but for serious impact, first wrap it in the target's dirty underpants, wetted with her urine, then encase it in aluminum foil, shiny side in. Be prepared to tell God why you did such a mean thing to her.

KEEP A MAN, LOSE A MAN

If your man threatens to leave you and you want him to stay, write his name on paper. Bore a hole in a Red Onion with a nail, roll the name paper tight, push it into the hole, and carry the Onion in your pocket to make him stay. If you ultimately decide that you want him gone, pull the paper out of the Onion, soak it in Four Thieves Vinegar, dress it with Red Pepper, reinsert it, and bury the Onion. When it rots, he will leave.

TO CAUSE SOMEONE TO SICKEN OR DIE

Write your enemy's name nine times on a paper. If the paper is also a handwriting sample of the enemy, it will be a better link. Wrap the paper around the enemy's hair, foot skin, nail clippings, or sexual fluids. Put it in a bottle with nine nails, nine pins, and nine needles. Add Crossing Powder, Goofer Dust, or Graveyard Dirt as appropriate. Bury the bottle at the enemy's doorstep where she will step over it.

TO CURSE AN ENEMY THIRTEEN WAYS

Four Thieves Vinegar is both protective and destructive; here it is used to sour an enemy's fortune. Write your enemy's name on brown paper with Dragon's Blood Ink and cross it out with a big black X. Wrap the name paper around a whole dried Red Pepper and tie it with black thread. Submerge this packet into a jar of Four Thieves Vinegar and close the jar. For 13 successive nights during the Waning Moon, burn a black candle dressed with Crossing Oil upside down on the lid of the jar, always starting at an hour when both hands of the clock are falling (e.g. from 12:01 to 12:29, from 1:01 to 1:29, etc.). As you light the candle, speak aloud 13 fully justified curses, in your own words, such as *"[Name], as God is my defender, may your fortune run out; [Name], as God is my defender, may your mind wander and weaken; [Name], as God is my defender, may your family abandon you; [Name], as God is my defender, may you go to jail for the crimes you have committed; [Name], as God is my defender, may everything in your life that was sweet turn as sour as this vinegar"* — up to a total of 13. It may help to write the 13 curses down and memorize them before you begin. Burn one candle per night, letting the wax from each candle build up on the jar's lid and sides. If you want to keep it going, stop after 13 days, wait out the period of the Waxing Moon, and begin working again when the Moon wanes.

7 DEADLY BIBLE PSALMS TO QUELL YOUR FOES

I wrote this list for my colleagues and clients at HoodooPsychics.com. It has proven very popular and i hope you find it useful as well. Even religious people have enemies, suffer oppression, and need relief from cruelty. God has inspired some very serious prayers in the form of Psalms which can be written out as prayer papers, burned to make Bible ashes, or dissolved into food or drink given to an enemy while casting justified curses. Known as the "imprecatory Psalms," these portions of scripture are powerful, effective, and definitely not to be trifled with!

- **Psalms 1:** *"The ungodly [...] are like the chaff which the wind driveth away [...] the way of the ungodly shall perish."* This Psalm removes unworthy and ungodly people from any group.
- **Psalms 37:** *"The arms of the wicked shall be broken [...] their sword shall enter into their own heart [and] the wicked shall perish [...] as the fat of lambs, [...] into smoke shall they consume away."* This cursing Psalm invokes physical injury and brings death by sword and fire to evil people.
- **Psalms 55:15:** *"Let death take my enemies by surprise; let them go down alive to the grave."* Here is a simple, direct, and right-to-the-point destruction Psalm. What's more, it asks God to give your enemies no warning, but to kill them unawares.
- **Psalms 58:6:** *"O God, break the teeth in their mouths."* Talk about specialized curses! This Psalm sends your enemies, especially gossipers, liars, and false tale-bearers, directly to the dentist!
- **Psalms 59:12:** *"For the sin of their mouth and the words of their lips let them be taken in their pride: and for cursing and lying which they speak."* God really hates liars, and this Psalm asks for particular curses to fall upon those who spread falsehoods or speak with arrogance or pride, or use foul language.
- **Psalms 109:8:** *"Let his days be few; and let another take his office."* Do you need to remove a bad politician or government official from your life? This is the Psalm to do it!
- **Psalms 137:9:** *"How blessed will be the one who seizes your infants and dashes them against the rocks!"* Finally, here is a terrible curse of vengeance that draws down God's ire upon entire families and employs military means to do so. Be careful with this one, folks — it's scary!

A NAME PAPER TO MOVE SOMEONE AWAY

In 1939, on his second trip to Memphis, Tennessee, Rev. Harry Hyatt interviewed a professional conjure doctor nicknamed "Ready Money" whom he called "The Mojo Expert" (Informant # 1534). Born in Baton Rouge, Louisiana, this man described how to drive someone out of town, using a combination of religious, herbal, and magical techniques that seamlessly integrated elements of European Pagan folk magic, Spiritualist Church magic, African folk magic, and Christian folk magic:

On a piece of paper, write out a cross comprised of your name as a short, horizontal line crossing the other man's name as a long, vertical line. Say *"God the Father, Son, and the Holy Ghost"* as you draw the cross.

```
            T
            H
            E
YOUR  N A M E
            O
            T
            H
            E
            R
            N
            A
            M
            E
```

Place one to two tablespoons of rain water that was caught in May, that is, May Day water, in a vial. Roll up the name paper and place it in the vial.

Next you will need dirt from a sinner-man's grave who died less than six months ago. To acquire it, dig wrist deep over his bosom or heart and extract three tablespoons (or one ounce). Put five pennies in the hole to buy that dirt and cover the hole.

Take the dirt home and mix it with Cayenne Pepper. Put half of it into the vial with the name paper and rain water, but save the rest. Bury the vial in the ground. (He does not say where, but it would be buried upside down and off your property, for the other person to step over.) Do this at 9:00 o'clock, 11:00 o'clock, or 2:00 o'clock, AM or PM, your choice.

Then go to a hardware store and buy a file, a regular triangular, three-sided file. Get a piece of lump Sulphur or Brimstone the size of the tip joint of your finger, about an inch long. Place a knife blade flat on it and pound it. To do this, wrap it in a cloth, and hit it with an iron, like an old cast-iron laundry iron. Mix into the Sulphur the rest of the Graveyard Dirt and Cayenne Pepper and put it all in a paper.

Go to his house and pour out the mixture from the paper, marking the direction he is to go. Use a metal rod to poke an angled hole in the ground, pointing in that direction, then stick the file into the angled hole, naming it for him, and hammer it in completely as you call his name and tell him exactly when to leave and where to go. In three days he will be gone.

BIBLIOGRAPHY

The Holy Bible: King James Version, Revised Edition. Thomas Nelson, Inc., 1976.

ARMAND, Khi. *Deliverance!* Missionary Independent Spiritual Church, 2015.

BETZ, Hans Dieter. *Greek Magical Papyri in Translation, Including the Demotic Spells.* University of Chicago Press, 1986.

DE CLAREMONT, Lewis. *Legends of Incense, Herb, and Oil Magic.* Oracle Publishing, 1936; Lucky Mojo Curio Co., 2016.

GAGER, John G. *Curse Tablets and Binding Spells of the Ancient World.* Oxford University Press, 1992.

GAMACHE, Henri. *Mystery of the Long Lost 8th, 9th and 10th Books of Moses.* Sheldon, 1948.

----------. *The Master Book of Candle Burning.* Dorene Publishing, 1942.

----------. *The Master Key to Occult Secrets.* Open Door Publishing Company, 1945.

GÅRDBÄCK, Johannes. *Trolldom:* Yronwode Institution for the Preservation and Popularization of Indigenous Ethnomagicology, 2015.

HASKINS, Jim. *Voodoo and Hoodoo.* Scarborough House, 1978.

HOHMAN, [Johann Georg]. *Pow-Wows or The Long Lost Friend.* Stein, 1935. [Reprints *The Long Secreted Friend.* John George Hohman, 1846].

HURSTON, Zora Neale. *Hoodoo in America.* Journal of American Folklore, Vol. 44, 1931.

----------. *Mules and Men.* J.B. Lippincott, 1935. Reprinted, Harper Collins, 1990.

HYATT, Harry Middleton. *Folklore From Adams County, Illinois.* Memoirs of the Alma Egan Hyatt Foundation, 1935; revised 2nd ed.1965.

----------. *Hoodoo–Conjuration–Witchcraft–Rootwork.* [Five Vols.] Memoirs of the Alma Egan Hyatt Foundation, 1970–78.

JOHNSON, F. Roy. *The Fabled Doctor Jim Jordan.* Johnson Publishing Co., 1963.

LAFOREST, Aura. *Hoodoo Spiritual Baths.* Lucky Mojo Curio Co., 2014.

LONG, Carolyn Morrow. *Spiritual Merchants.* University of Tennessee Press, 2001.

MATHERS, Samuel Liddell MacGregor. *The Key of Solomon the King (Clavicula Salomonis).* George Redway, 1888.

MICHÆLE, Miss and Prof. Charles Porterfield. *Hoodoo Bible Magic.* Missionary Independent Spiritual Church, 2014.

MILLETT, Deacon. *Hoodoo Honey and Sugar Spells.* Lucky Mojo Curio Co., 2013.

----------. *Hoodoo Return and Reconciliation Spells.* Lucky Mojo Curio Co., 2015.

[MOSES; attributed] *The Sixth and Seventh Books of Moses.* Wehman Brothers, 1880. [translated from the German edition of 1865 published by Johann Scheible.]

PETERSON, Joseph. *The Sixth and Seventh Books of Moses.* Ibis Press, 2008.

PORTERFIELD, Charles. *A Deck of Spells.* Lucky Mojo Curio Co., 2015.

PUCKETT, Newbell Niles. *Folk Beliefs of the Southern Negro.* University of North Carolina Press, 1926.

SELIG, Godfrey. *Secrets of the Psalms.* [n.p.], [c. 1788].

SONNY BOY [pseudonym]. *King Solomon's Alleged Guide to Success? Power!* Sonny Boy Products, [c.1960].

SPAMER, Adolf. *Die Deutsche Volkskunde.* Herbert Steubenrauch, 1935.

TRACHTENBERG, Joshua. *Jewish Magic and Superstition.* Behrman's Jewish Book House, 1939.

YRONWODE, Catherine. *Hoodoo Herb and Root Magic.* Lucky Mojo Curio Co., 2002.

---------- *The Lucky W Amulet Archive.* LuckyMojo.com/luckyw.html 1994 - 2015.

---------- and Mikhail Strabo [Sydney J. R. Steiner]. *The Art of Hoodoo Candle Magic.* Missionary Independent Spiritual Church, 2013.

---------- et al. *The Black Folder.* Missionary Independent Spiritual Church, 2013.